THE POINT OF NO RETURN

Yvonne Cardogna

Order this book online at www.trafford.com
or email orders@trafford.com

Most Trafford titles are also available at major online book retailers.

Print information available on the last page.

ISBN: 978-1-6987-1636-7 (sc)
ISBN: 978-1-6987-1638-1 (hc)
ISBN: 978-1-6987-1637-4 (e)

Library of Congress Control Number: 2024902699

Trafford rev. 02/02/2024

 www.trafford.com

North America & international
toll-free: 844-688-6899 (USA & Canada)
fax: 812 355 4082

To my family, for they are my home.

The Point of No Return is a continuation of the Island
of the Elyms, a book about the Sicilian way of life
inspired by passion, mystery, and enchantment.

The voyage through Sicily is now happily completed and will
for me be an indestructible treasure for my whole life.

—F.W. Goethe

ACKNOWLEDGMENTS

Many people have been part of my life. First of all, my family has offered support and guidance. I am, to say the least, surrounded by talented people who take away the loneliness of being a writer.

There are so many things I can say about my wonderful family. From the youngest to the oldest, God blesses my family, sowing grace and strengthening our relationship, weaving love into my work.

I am grateful to my family:
Elvira Edwards
Jeff Edwards
Teresa Michael
Hannah Meenan
John Meenan
Sarah Edwards-Loughton
Andrew Loughton
Great-grandchildren

A great friendship is when people know all about you but like you anyway.

Sue Wallwork
Donna Di Camillo
Mary McAlleer
Francine Cartaginese
Joan Recontre

CONTENTS

Start by doing what's necessary; then do what's possible; and suddenly you are doing the impossible.

—St. Francis of Assisi

My mother had finished packing. Her wishes had come true. I, on the other hand, looking out from our villa in Messina, realized that my life, as I knew it, was ending. Will I ever again see the beautiful place where I was born?

Our villa was behind the "Holy Mountain" (Monte Santo). As we admired Messina's port, we saw a huge ship in the distance. As it came closer, we could see the name on the ship, Australia.

As I turned toward my mother, I realized that she knew the Australia was going to the Australian oceans. We soon had to leave for our journey, which was paved with uncertainty and mystery.

As we left, sadness and tears filled the air.

Vos et ipsam civitatem benedicimus. We bless you and your city.[1]

1

THE JOURNEY BEGINS

The waves lapped softly on the flanks of the ship—the only sound in the quietness and stillness of the night. The atmosphere of peacefulness was in direct contrast to the turmoil within me. Until a few months ago, my future appeared mapped out, and I simply had to walk into it and claim it. Unexpectedly, though, I was faced with this drastic change that brought with it an ocean of uncertainty and demanded supreme endurance and sacrifice. Would I have the strength to survive?

So, this was the nefarious destiny predicted at my birth, interpreted by soothsayers because of the fact that my first glimpse of the world was sidewise and by the blast of the colorful pyrotechnics that shook the city in its foundation. It was not unusual for Sicily to shake from the earthquakes caused by the eruptions of the volcano Etna. In fact, Sicily, because it shook frequently, was called l'Isola Ballerina (the dancing island), and hence, people, accustomed as they were, did not take much notice when the shaking of their city was caused by the deafening explosion of bombs for religious purposes. One might say that my birth was literally an explosive event.

All of this was happening simultaneously: the appearance of the statue of the Madonna of the Sacred Letter at the door of the Cathedral of Messina and the faithful greeting the statue with a thunderous applause. The brass band was playing and making a racket. Then there was the explosion of the firework bombs.

Amid all of this, my mother's screeching labor cries became louder in order to be heard, not to mention the commotion made by the room full of people who were witnessing my birth. What an ambience for my appearance into the world! An unbelievable clamor of sounds, conflicting opinions, and strong convictions were to greet me.

I must have been bewildered and would, no doubt, have turned back from whence I came if in all the chaos I had not lost my way. But I had better become accustomed quickly, for the confusion that confronted me was to be the norm and not the exception in Casa Del Feo. And so it had been with my life until this morning—confused and bewildered. Yet, I felt I was saner than the rest of my family. This last endeavor definitely proved it.

Even if it seemed a lifetime ago, it was only this morning that I was standing on the balcony of our villa in Messina pondering the situation that confronted me. I was still hoping for a thunderous bolt from the mighty Zeus to awaken me from the nightmare I was having. But none came, since I was actually living my incubus. It had been a day filled with emotions, and suddenly I felt drained. It was as if every ounce of energy had been siphoned out of my body. With apathy and stolidity, I looked around and realized that only a few solitary figures remained on deck. They looked as lonely and as lost as I did.

Perhaps they were also dragged away from their home against their will, I thought to myself sadly.

It was not quite accurate to say that I had been "dragged away against my will," though, since I was not supposed to have a will. No Sicilian girl, under the power of the omnipotent and omniscient—that is, the all-knowing parents—ever could or should allow herself to have a will. My opinion was considered so minuscule that it could be defined as insignificant, pointless, and worthless and hence to be absolutely and positively ignored. So, not only was I not consulted on a decision that would upend my life; no one cared that any vision and dreams I may have had for my own future had ended as abruptly and as finitely as a sudden death.

If that sounds as if most Sicilian parents look down on their children with a disciplinarian God's-eye view, then perhaps I should clarify that I believed God, in his infinite goodness, looked upon his children with a merciful eye. My parents had shown no mercy. Was I angry? Yes, I was angry. Was my anger an exercise in futility? Of course, it was! No one really cared.

I felt I had been torn from my roots and left a frail little sapling. Planted in a foreign land, the little sapling would be deciduous, and when spring came, there would be no frondescence. It would be predisposed to the change of the elements. Now swaying in the wind, now subjected to the shivering cold, and now burned under the hot Australian sun. Finally, there would be no growth, and the little sapling would die.

"This sapling is dead because it has no roots," they would lament. But then, because of its insignificance, the sapling would be discarded. "Poor, poor little fledgling." I sobbed, feeling lost in the middle of the mysterious and immense sea—the breadth and depth of which was incomprehensible to me.

Deep in thought, I glanced at the horizon, but to my bewilderment, there wasn't one. It seemed as if the ship were enclosed in a huge black hole—an enormous balloon out of which there was no escape. It was as if the pitch-black sea and the raven sky symbolized my future—a future without vision. This was the darkest and the most forlorn night I had ever experienced.

Suddenly, I was abruptly extricated from my thoughts by a powerful presence. I sensed that the two baronesses were standing behind me. As I turned to face them, I knew instantly that Mamma and Nonna were not too pleased with me. No doubt I would be reprimanded for some indiscretion or other I had committed. They were standing there, with their hands on their hips, looking like two generals ready to send their troops to the front line. But there weren't any troops—there was only me.

"What would your father say if he saw you all alone in the dark?" said Mother, always bringing Papà into the equation, as if she didn't have a mind of her own.

"He will say nothing unless you tell him, since he is thousands of miles away," I retorted. There was hostility in my voice.

Mother, in this unfortunate episode, had been single-minded and totally self-absorbed. Most of the time, Mother was self-involved. Nonna, on the other hand, had seemed a little compassionate toward me, as if she understood my plight. Not that she would say so, though, because parents and grandparents had to gang together and show a united front to their children and grandchildren for fear they would rebel and become mutinous and insubordinate toward their high-ranking position that had been vested to them by a supreme power.

I resented being treated like a subservient, inconspicuous child, since I thought I had demonstrated that I was quite mature by taking adult responsibilities. I had proven it many times when I had rescued my mother from her own fears and insecurities, and when I had taken up the duties of overseeing the many tasks and demands of our enormous estate, duties that were the earmark of the Sicilian landowners. The rather sad episodes in my mother's life had left an indelible scar on her mind. On the surface, she appeared as if she had dealt with her anxieties, but I knew she had not and feared one day they would surface. If and when that happens, what is it going to happen to Mother? I was afraid for her.

"Hurry up and come to bed, Marianna!" was mother's stern command. The harsh and aggressive sound in her voice was an attempt to exercise her power.

People with insecurities usually adopt a peremptory tone, I told myself. But since I did not desire to have a confrontation with Mother, I acquiesced and went down to the cabin. On the way to the cabin, Mother mumbled something—some warning, no doubt, but I was too exhausted both physically and emotionally to pay much attention.

Carolina and I shared a two-berth cabin, while Mamma and Nonna occupied the one adjacent to ours. When I entered the cabin, Carolina was already asleep; I undressed quietly in the dark, careful not to wake her. Hoping for some sleep that would induce, if not restfulness, at least some sort of insensibleness, I went to bed. I tossed and turned for a while, but then exhausted by the longest day of my whole life, I fell into a restless slumber. My sleep was crowded with erratic dreams, but in the morning, I could not recall any of them.

"Marianna, if you want to remember your dreams, you should not scratch your head," Carmela would have said in a matter-of-fact way.

Apparently, the scratching of one's head after dreaming made the dream disappear. Almost similar to Dante's immersion in the waters of the Lethe, which caused him oblivion and forgetfulness from his past sins, I thought to myself with a hint of a smile, forgetting for an instant my own sadness. "Don't be absurd, Carmela." I would have replied in a petulant way.

"Don't be what?"

"Don't be absurd—your tales are preposterous."

"You change a difficult word with a more difficult one," Carmela would have replied, throwing a pot from a distance and making a hell of a racket. "Can't you speak in plain Sicilian, Marianna?"

The thought of Carmela brought a smile to my lips and tears to my eyes. Would she survive the pain and the sense of loss she would have felt with our departure? Would I see her again? My heart sank as something within me told me with a violent certainty that I would not.

2

THE FIRST MORNING
ON THE AUSTRALIA

The following morning, as I was accustomed to do since childhood, I arose early. I tiptoed out of the cabin to go on deck. There were only a few people around, mostly members of the crew.

"Buon giorno, Signorina," greeted one of them, lifting his cap.

"Buon giorno," I replied without much enthusiasm.

"You're up early this morning, Signorina," continued the man affably, stating the obvious.

"Yes," I replied. There was a hint of annoyance in my voice, as I preferred to be left alone.

As I reached the deck, dawn was breaking, and with it last night's eerie atmosphere had vanished. The horizon had shifted somewhat, and one could see some distance away. Yet sea and sky surrounded us and the feeling of being held captive remained. I could not bring myself to go toward the bow of the ship. It was as if I would be forced to gaze into this unknown, frightening, and nugatory life that I was destined to have.

As I was heading toward the stern, I hoped for a glimpse of something—anything which up to now had been constant in my life. The only thing I could see, though, was the trail of frothy water left behind by the ship as it cut through it with amazing velocity. So fast, in fact, that paradoxically it felt as if it were standing still. This country called Australia must be situated at the end of the world if this enormous vessel, at the speed which it travels, takes nearly a month to arrive, I thought to myself, fully aware that the farther away the ship took us from our home, the more difficult it would be for us to return. At least not in the immediate future, if ever.

"People who go past the Pillars of Hercules will never return," Carmela would have said, unaware that she, more or less, was quoting the great poet, Dante.

> I and my fellows were grown old and tardy
> Or ere we made the straits where Hercules
> Set up his marks, that none should prove so hardy
> To venture the uncharted distances …
> (Dante, Inferno: Canto XXVI)

It was the Strait of Gibraltar where Hercules, according to legend, had placed the limits beyond which man was not permitted to cross or explore. But Ulysses, as stated in Dante's Inferno, ignoring the principle, unwisely and hazardously had crossed over the boundary, and with great peril, had sailed the "uncharted distances." Our route on the Australia was, obviously, a different one. We were not going through the Strait of Gibraltar, but through the Suez Canal. Fully aware that our course was "charted," as were most seas, I still could not help wondering if we also had a limit, if not an unexplored periphery—a point of no return.

Was this point of no return beyond the Suez Canal? Was it in the Red Sea? Or was it in the Indian Ocean? Who knows? I told myself, shrugging my shoulders, furious for allowing Carmela to influence my thoughts. Yet her words, spoken with conviction, kept on haunting me: "People who go to Australia never come back."

"Buon giorno, Signorina," said a young woman in a soft voice.

"Buon giorno," I replied, almost glad to have a young companion who would somehow constrain my erratic thoughts and arrest my wandering mind.

The young woman looked at me, at first hesitantly, but then taking courage. She said, "I saw you yesterday as you and your family came on board ship. You looked so sad and unhappy. If you don't mind my asking, why were you distressed? Didn't you want to go to Australia? Don't you want to visit another land?"

"We are not visiting another land, are we? We are going as migrants," I said with sarcasm.

"Yes, I know, but surely, we will be treated with respect since it was at the invitation of the Australian government that we are migrating. Apparently, they need skilled people to help build the country." There was a hint of hope in the young woman's voice.

"I hope you're right. I personally have a vision of a future filled with indignity and humiliation," I said. As soon as I spoke, I regretted my prophecy of doom, for I realized that my feelings of dejection would discourage the young woman. "I'm sorry, I didn't mean to be so pessimistic," I said sincerely. Changing the subject, I stretched out my hand and said, "My name is Marianna. What's yours"?

"Lina," she replied simply, shaking my hand. I turned to look at her. She was an attractive girl, slender with long black hair. Her eyes seemed gray in the first light of dawn. She was a little older than I was.

"Where do you come from, Lina"? I asked.

"From the Aeolian Islands. I come from the island of Salina, to be exact." I thought I saw tears in her eyes, but in the pale, early-morning light, I wasn't sure.

"Are you traveling with your family"? Now I was certain that there were tears in her eyes.

"No," she sobbed, "I'm all alone. I left my family behind—my mother and father, three sisters, and two brothers.

What could a young girl be doing all alone? How could her family let her migrate to another country? I thought, bewildered. Out loud, I said, "Do you have a job in Australia"?

"No," replied Lina with a sigh, "I have a husband."

"You look too young to be married." I was perplexed.

"I am young, but I come from a poor family and there wasn't enough food for all of us, especially after the war. So, this man saw my photograph that a friend who has migrated to Australia had. Wanting to settle down, he asked for my hand in marriage. My family accepted for me."

"Your family accepted for you? Haven't you met this man?" I was shocked.

"Not in person, no. We exchanged photographs. He seems a handsome man, though."

"But you said you were married. How could you be married if you haven't met him?"

"We were married by proxy."

Dawn was breaking, and I could see her face clearly now. She was quite beautiful. Any man would be proud to have her as his wife. Poor girl, she is sacrificing so much, I thought to myself with a deep sense of compassion. "What does a proxy marriage involve?" I asked.

"There's a ceremony the same as any other marriage except that another person stands in for the groom. You make the usual promises: to respect, love, and obey, and then you are declared married."

"But how can you make such promises and keep them when you don't even know the man?" I was appalled at such an archaic and barbaric practice.

"Oh, I will keep my promises which I made before God. I will respect, love, and obey my husband," said the girl with conviction.

But will he respect, love, and obey you? Or will he use you as someone who cooks his meals, washes his clothes, and raises his children? I thought to myself, feeling offended for this woman and for the other women in the same predicament. However, I could not voice my opinion to this girl; her life would be hard enough without my adding to the insecurities and fears she must be feeling.

"There have been men who have requested a wife," continued Lina, "and then sent the young woman someone else's photograph—a photograph of a younger or a more handsome man. When the wife meets the husband for the first time, she realizes that the man she married is not the one in the photograph. By then it's too late, of course."

"Are you sure your husband is the same person as the one in the photo?" I asked.

"Yes, my friend has attested to his honesty. She assures me that he is a kind, hardworking, and good-looking man."

I was not able to approve or understand the concept of "requesting a wife." The principle of entering into marriage by proxy, in my opinion, was the same to that of an encounter between a bull with a cow for the basic purpose for the bull to impregnate the cow. Actually, it was much worse, since the bull and the cow, once the aim was accomplished, parted their ways, perhaps, to meet again another year.

Instead, the couple who entered into a proxy marriage, unlike the cow and the bull, was stuck with one another for the duration. The husband, being the master, tired from a day's work, would demand attention, and the loyal wife, in her subservient role, would satisfy his every whim. Maybe I'm a little too cynical—maybe these contractual unions work, if for no other reason than the fact that the alternative is worse—the dreaded poverty, I thought.

Thinking of bulls, cows, and proxy marriages, I had almost forgotten that Lina was still standing there and was silently staring at me. I felt compelled to say something, so I stated the obvious. "So you come from Salina."

"Yes," replied Lina.

"I believe it's a beautiful place."

"Yes, it is." It was evident Lina was already missing her enchanting little island.

"I wish I had seen it before I left Sicily. Actually, I wish I had seen all the seven sisters of the whole Aeolian archipelago—the seven jewels of the Mediterranean, as they're called," I said with a sigh. "But then," I continued, "I have not seen much of Sicily either."

"We will … one day we will see it. I know I will return. I must! I must see my family again," said Lina, sobbing.

"Yes, we will go back, I'm certain,", I reassured Lina, placing my arm around her shoulders to console her. Deep down, however, I was far from certain. I cannot be certain because the decision does not depend on me, I thought with a sense of helplessness. Turning to Lina, I said, "Lina, tell me about Salina."

"Salina was called Didyme, which means twin, by the Greeks. It was called that because there are two mountains that, join in the valley. Salina has a small lake where the sea salt is harvested. There are also the ruins of walls built by imperial Rome. Salina, contrary to the other islands of the archipelago, is quite green because it has fresh water. As a result, there are fruit trees, vineyards, and the cultivation of capers. The island's highest peak is 963 meters, above sea level. Actually, Salina is higher than the other islands," said Lina, staring in the distance as if she was seeing what she was describing.

"We can see the Aeolian Islands from Sicily," I uttered softly so as not to disturb Lina's vision.

"Can you"?

"Yes."

"Yes, of course you can," added Lina quickly, as if shaken into reality from her daydreaming. "Of course, you can see the islands in the same way as we can see Sicily. How silly of me."

"Carmela used to say that if we saw the Aeolian Islands clearly, it would mean rain. It never failed, every time we saw them sharply silhouetted against the sky, it would, indeed, rain. Of course, I never told Carmela I believed what she was saying. In fact, in order to irritate her a little, I pretended she was speaking nonsense. I loved to see her upset; she would let out a litany of colorful words, directed at me."

"You are a spoiled child, and you keep on reading all those books to learn stuff so that you can annoy me." Carmela would say, flicking her unruly hair with the back of the hand, which I used to call "cockscomb."

"No, I'm not spoiled, and most assuredly, I'm not a child," would be my adamant reply.

"Most, what? There you go again, practicing all those funny words you read in books on me."

I was visualizing the events in the kitchen of Casa Del Feo. And like Lina, I was hoping I would once again experience those unforgettable moments with those people I had left behind. But with each mile that the ship traveled and with each moment that passed by, the people we loved, in spite of all their peculiarities, were becoming progressively more distant. Distant from our sight, but never distant from our hearts and minds. I vowed to myself.

Now it was Lina who, out of reverence, did not want to disturb my memories, which like hers were sacred to me. We stood there, a lump in our throat, and our eyes filled with tears. All the dear faces of the people I loved, as if surfacing from the depths of the sea, were floating past me. There was Sara, whose ancient wisdom I admired; she had taught me so much about popular culture. There was her husband, Peppe, whose face and skin had been plowed and furrowed by the elements; he seemed as perennial and as timeless as the universe. Peppe had demonstrated to me the existence of unconditional love.

There were all the children and the wives of the campieri and of the coloni, who looked after our enormous estate, and who awaited my visits with anticipation and excitement. But there would be no more visits and no more sweet treats for those children who waited patiently, sitting on the doorstep of their homes. But above all there was Basilio, who had the misfortune to be the illegitimate grandson of my promiscuous grandfather whom, to my mother's delight and to my outmost disgust, I would undoubtedly meet for the first time in Australia.

Poor Basilio! I was grateful that we had been able to break the silence, which had lasted for a few generations. We had chosen to break the omertà which, being the Sicilian hallmark, was something people did not do lightly, if at all. Secrets were whispered in the dim light of a room, and usually taken to the grave. As far as I knew, Carmela was the only one who could hear behind solid wooden doors and thick walls.

I must have whispered the names of all the people dear to me out aloud, because Lina asked, "Marianna, who is Carmela, and who are Sara, Peppe, and Basilio?"

I could not bring myself to tell Lina that those people were the coloni and the servants of Baronessa Camilla, my grandmother, and Baronessa Eleonora, my mother. "They are members of my family," I said simply. As far as I was concerned, I was telling the truth. Just then, we were called in to breakfast.

3

THE SUEZ CANAL

"The captain has invited us to dine with him," said Nonna.

"Make sure you don't wander around and stray away, as usual," added Mother.

These people are still delusional, I thought to myself. They still act as if they are on a holiday cruise that will last only a few weeks. Out loud, I replied with vehemence, "You make me sound like a puppy dog. We are on a ship, for heaven's sake. Even on this floating Brobdingnagian monster, my wandering is somewhat limited, wouldn't you say? How far do you think I can stray? Maybe you should put me on a leash."

"There are many dangers everywhere for a young girl," Mother declared convincingly.

There were times when every shadow and every sound made Mother feel apprehensive and vulnerable. A few times I had noticed one of her old faraway looks, as if she were lost in a moment in time, a moment so shattering that was able to hold her hostage.

"Mamma! Mamma!" I would call out, but there would be no response. "Mamma! Do you hear me?" I would shake her gently until she was released from her little demon that had a paralyzing power over her. Those times, my heart would fill with compassion and tenderness.

I went on deck and heard a child shout to his mother, "Look Mamma, we've arrived."

"No," replied the mother, "this is only a port of call. It will be a long time before we arrive at our destination."

"Where is your destination? If you don't mind my asking," I inquired.

"Sydney." She replied, "What about yours?"

"Fremantle."

"Are we going ashore?" The young boy was tugging at his mother's hand.

"No, darling. Not this time."

"Why not?"

"Because we won't be stopping for too long."

"We can go down for a little while," insisted the boy.

"No," repeated the mother. "You don't want the ship to leave us behind, do you?"

"No," the boy sounded disappointed. But since the prospect of being left behind must have been terrifying to him, he reluctantly gave up on the idea.

"Port Said!" someone announced, one of the crew, I suspected. "We have arrived at Port Said," he repeated.

Everyone was on deck, and each person, either by pushing or shoving, was trying to claim a spot by the railing. In the distance, I saw Lina approaching and signaled her to join me. She somehow managed to squeeze in next to me.

"How are you, Marianna? Are you feeling better today?" asked Lina with a slight suggestion of a smile.

"Yes, and you?" I tried to smile back at her, but since my facial features had been fixed in the same sad demeanor for days, it was difficult, if not impossible to smile. I felt sure that my face resembled —hardness, that is—that statue of the head of Aphrodite of the fourth and fifth century BC, kept in the museum in the town

Erice, the land of the ancient Elyms. The only way to soften my face would be with a clout of a sledgehammer, which in all probability would crack it rather than soften it.

While, as usual, I was confabulating with myself in a disorderly way with my imaginary experiences, at times believing them to be true, the crew was trying to dock the ship. There were ropes everywhere, and people were tripping over them to try and see the port of call.

"Please let us finish berthing the ship, and then you can look as much as you want," growled a member of the crew, who was trying to maneuver thick ropes and becoming more impatient by the minute.

When the ship finally docked, everyone rushed to see what was waiting on the shore of a different continent. There were people everywhere; they were trying to sell colorful materials, beads, and other merchandise.

"Port Said is the northern terminal of the Suez Canal. It has a harbor protected by that mole, which is about three miles long," said the young crew member, pointing with his index finger toward the mole. I had noticed the young man staring at me a few times when he thought I was not watching and looking quickly away when my gaze turned toward him. He was obviously rather shy. He was fairly good looking with curly black hair, which was usually squashed by the sailor's cap he wore. He was of a slim build and of medium height. When he smiled, two cute dimples appeared on his cheeks.

"Thank you for the lesson. This is all new and very interesting to me." I replied, stretching out my hand toward the dock.

"I thought it might be." The young man looked pleased with himself. He was looking around cautiously as if worried about his superiors spotting him talking to me.

Probably he is not permitted to fraternize with the passengers, I thought to myself. I had to admit that touching another continent filled me with both fascination and apprehension. On the one hand, my geography map was coming to life, and on the other, we were gaining distance from the only home I had ever known.

As we entered the Suez Canal, we were leaving the Mediterranean Sea behind and entering the Red Sea. I wondered if Hercules, or some other mythological hero, had also been in this particular spot.

The narrow passage of the Suez Canal could be comparable to the two mountains on the opposite sides of the western entrance to the Mediterranean through which Hercules had sailed in a floating cup, could they not? I asked myself, being aware and, at the same time, horrified of how powerful Carmela's brainwashing had been. I knew, however, with certainty, that there would be a spot, physical, psychological, or spiritual, from which there would be no return. Perhaps, the Indian Ocean?

"The Suez Canal," continued the young sailor, whose presence I had temporarily forgotten, "connects the Mediterranean Sea with the Gulf of Suez and from then on with the Red Sea." He was obviously eager to impress.

"How long is the canal?" I asked with interest.

"About 160 kilometers," replied the young man, no doubt delighted that he had aroused my curiosity.

"The canal was planned by the French engineer Ferdinand Lesseps. The work began in 1859 near Port Said. On the November 17, 1869, the waters of the Mediterranean flowed into the Red Sea."

"That must have been very exciting," I stated.

"Yes, it was," replied the young man, furtively looking around to see if anyone was watching him. I followed his gaze and noticed I was being stared at by two aristocratic figures, namely my mother and grandmother, whose imposing demeanor overshadowed everyone else. Their disapproving glance told me, in no uncertain terms, that they thought talking to the sailor was considered inappropriate and hence my reputation would be tarnished. I personally did not believe that conversation between two civilized people was either immoral or sinful, so I ignored both of them and continued my conversation with the sailor. No doubt I would hear later the litany of reasons why I should not speak to men.

"The termination of the Suez Canal was the cause of splendid celebrations here in Port Said. It appears that the lavish event began with spectacular fireworks followed by a ball attended by six thousand people. Among them there were many heads of state, including the Emperor of Austria, the Empress Eugenie, the Prince of Wales, the Prince of Prussia, and the Prince of the Netherlands."

"Oh! How exciting! It must have been an impressive occasion," I exclaimed. The sailor had captured my imagination, and I was visualizing the ladies dressed in glamorous evening gowns and looking beautiful. They floated and swayed gracefully as they danced with their partners to the music of a tango or a waltz. The gentlemen, looking very dashing, slightly brushed the ladies' cheeks with their own. Perhaps they whispered a compliment, discussed the affairs of the state, or promised to sign a treaty, to be forgotten the following morning.

"For the occasion," continued the sailor, "two convoys of ships entered the canal from the northern and southern points and met here at Ismailia. Apparently, the celebrations continued for weeks, which also marked the opening of Cairo's Opera House."

"Thank you so much for the history lesson. I will never forget it," I said enthusiastically. Then remembering that we had not been introduced, I added, "By the way, my name is Marianna, what's yours?"

"Guido," he replied shyly.

"Piacere, Guido," I said, shaking his hand. As soon as I did that, I realized that his superiors could reprimand him for socializing with the passengers.

"Piacere mio, Signorina Marianna," he whispered.

Guido excused himself because the time had come to weigh anchor, and he was needed to maneuver all those thick ropes. The passengers on deck were politely told to move down to the big salon until the ship had sailed. I spotted Nonna and Mamma walking directly toward me. I tried to change direction, but to no avail. Before I could detour, they had planted themselves in front of me, obstructing my way with their awesome and intimidating presence. By their disgruntled gape, I knew I was in for a telling off.

"Marianna, when will you ever learn?" said mother with an accusative tone.

"Learn what?" I replied, pretending not to understand what she was saying.

"You must know there are hidden dangers in every corner for a young lady like you," added Nonna in a more amiable tone.

"There aren't any dangers on a boat, especially when there are crew members in every corner of it to make sure that the passengers are safe," I said with conviction.

"What makes you think you can trust the crew members?" retorted mother impatiently. "You know what happens if you are seen talking to male strangers?"

"Yes! I would lose my virginity." Mother became rigid and looked like an ambulatory cadaver or death warmed up.

"You are going to be the death of me, Marianna," said Mother.

"Until a few months ago I was 'the life of you' and now, suddenly, I am the death of you? There's no pleasing you, is there?"

"Marianna, please understand once and for all that once a girl loses her reputation, she will never recapture it," said Mother knowingly. Her voice sounded a little more docile. I looked at her and noticed a hint of color gradually coming back into her cheeks.

"Don't worry, Mamma, I may have lost my psychological virginity, but I will not lose my physical one." I looked at Mamma and Nonna, and this time, they both looked like corpses.

Mother gasped for air and finally emitted a huge sigh. She somehow found the strength to ask, "Please explain to me, what is a 'psychological virginity?'"

"A closed-mindedness." I replied, convinced that my family did not just have a closed mind, but a "locked mind." I think this time mother's sigh was one of relief.

While I was squabbling with my mother and grandmother, the ship had left Port Said and was carefully and slowly moving through the canal. As I looked in the distance, the Suez Canal seemed rather narrow for a huge vessel like ours. I feared it would not be able to go through it without scraping both sides of the canal. I soon realized, though, that I had misconceived the canal's width. The ship, navigating cautiously, gradually was able to make it through to the other side.

There was plenty of room after all, I thought.

My heart was welling up with sadness. We had left the Mediterranean behind. It was the last vestige of something I was familiar with. It was the sea that embraced my island as it lapped, at times gently and at times crashing against its shores with the fury of the angry Poseidon.

A silent tear, a melancholy sigh, and a cherished memory appeared to be everyone's burden. Suddenly, I thought I heard the screeching and the cacophonous sound of thick, rusty iron doors closing behind us. A shiver ran up and down my spine. Was this the point of no return? Had those doors closed forever? Was this my overactive imagination at play once again? "Perhaps—perhaps not," I whispered.

4

THE RED SEA

It was dawn; light was appearing on the horizon. Very soon the rays of the sun would shine on the water, giving it a rich, golden glow. It would glisten and sparkle like jewels. The mornings on the Australia were, indeed, spectacular. The people who danced the night away and stayed in bed until late morning are not aware of the breathtaking scene they're missing, I thought.

The sun was rising and expanding rapidly, and the day was breaking in all its magnificent glory. The water of the Red Sea, paradoxically, was a clear and dazzling brilliant blue. I looked around, and another early riser greeted me.

"Buon giorno, Marianna."

"Buon giorno, Lina."

"It's a beautiful sight, isn't it?" Lina outstretched her hands as if she wanted to encompass and embrace the sea.

"Yes, it is." For the first time there was excitement in my voice.

"You seem happier than you have been before. Are you becoming accustomed to the fact that soon you'll be visiting another country?" said Lina with a smile. Her face lit up, and her smile had softened her features, making her look quite attractive.

We Sicilians don't smile enough. We always think of the worst, I thought to myself. Out loud, I said, "In truth, it's not that I don't want to visit another country, for I had intention of traveling after I finished school. I simply did not want to be a migrant, because it seems to have a stigma attached to the very name."

"Why should there be a stigma to being a migrant?" Lina said, looking puzzled.

"I guess they think that people who migrate are illiterate and the poorest of the poor." I felt mortified at the thought.

"That's true, isn't it? About being poor I mean, not illiterate. There aren't any illiterate people anymore. It seems that when Mussolini was in power, he made going to school compulsory. At least that's what I heard," said Lina cautiously, looking around in case someone had heard her talk about the infamous dictator. People avoided mentioning his name, almost trying to obliterate history itself.

"Don't tell me Mussolini actually did something good?" I was incredulous.

"If making school compulsory, is the right thing to do, then he must have done at least one good thing," said Lina. "But tell me, are you feeling better about the prospect of going to Australia?"

"There's not much I can do now, is there? I guess, what was irreconcilable for me was the suddenness of our departure and the fact that I didn't have a choice in the matter. If I had had more time, who knows? Maybe, gradually, I could have accepted the idea," I said pensively.

"I don't think we have a choice in anything—actually, I am pretty sure we don't," Lina asserted.

"I've always believed that we have freedom of choice," I replied.

"Do you still think we do? Even though, for different reasons, we were forced to migrate? This only should prove to you that we don't have freedom of choice." Lina was adamant.

"If people would not exercise their power over others, which they have no right to do, then we would be able to choose." I spoke with conviction.

"Parents think they have the right to have power over their children, especially if the children happen to be girls. As for the husbands, they definitely think their wives' work is to please them—their masters." There was a tinge of bitterness in Lina's voice.

"I've always been of the opinion that people oppress other people because we allow them to. I have no intention of permitting my husband, if and when I marry, to be lord over me as if he were some supreme being," I said vehemently.

Lina laughed without reservation. When she finished her chortle, she said, "Surely, you must be joking. You ... you 'have no intention of permitting' your husband? Do you know what you're saying?"

"Yes, I do. My husband will treat me as his equal or else he can walk." I felt passionate about the subject.

"Marianna, you sound like one of those Sicilian baronesses. You know, one of those landowners who are wont to give orders to the lower-class peasants. Obviously, those people have power over the hardworking contadini. If it's not one person it's another who gives orders in Sicily." Lina's sigh sounded helpless.

"I've always had respect for people and have treated them as my equals, no matter their social status," I replied, without telling Lina that she was close to the truth. I felt that if I were to reveal to her the true identity of my family—the Del Feo barons of Sicily, she would somehow change toward me. Anyway, the name wasn't going to mean much in Australia, and it would not mean much to future Italian generations. Sicily, however, would hold on tight to its heritage and traditions.

"I guess, unless society's attitude changes, we will have people oppressing people. I for one will never tolerate being oppressed or abused by anyone," I said with conviction.

"What can we possibly do to change society's attitude?" Lina sounded perplexed.

"What I just said. We could start by treating one another with human concern and regard, giving people back their lost dignity and self-worth. As you know, the people of the Sicilian working class feel as though they deserve to be treated the way they do. I happen to think that no human being deserves to be treated less than a donkey."

"What you say, Marianna, has merit, but poor people cannot antagonize their masters by refusing to accept their command; their job is at stake and without work, there's no food on the table for the family." Lina sounded as if she knew what she was talking about. I felt compassion for her.

"Equality is not an easy thing to achieve, because people in power do not want to relinquish it, but it's not impossible. We may even see laws change in our lifetime, I'm certain. I feel positive we will," I said, trying to convince myself.

"You're a most unusual Sicilian, Marianna."

"So, I've been told. But I'm a Sicilian nevertheless."

"No doubt about it; your passion testifies to that. You almost make me believe that one day people will not have to crawl to their bosses and women will not have to be subjugated by their husbands." There was hope in Lina's voice.

"My vision for the future is that people will have a choice for what they want to do and what they want to be in life. And when that happens, we will finally have a just society." Changing the subject, I said, "I think we have missed our first turn for breakfast, we better go in if we don't want to miss it altogether. I'm ravenous."

Lina nodded. "So am I," she said.

As we went toward the enormous dining salon, I hoped my mother and grandmother had already been to breakfast, which meant I could be free from their disapproving stares. No such luck, though; they were there in all their contumelious glory seated at a table in a secluded corner. Their haughty attitude, while it might still have had a place in Sicily, was definitely out of place on a ship that was transporting migrants to a new land. I had hoped to sit with Lina and her friends; it would have been much more interesting. But it was too late; they looked around and spotted me and signaled me to join them. I excused myself from Lina and, reluctantly went toward them. The steward greeted me, bowing from the waist down

"Buon giorno, baronessina. Your mother, grandmother, and sister are sitting over there," he said, pointing to the table in the corner.

"Buon giorno. Yes, thank you. I can see them." Obviously, the captain had spread the word about my identity. I hope it doesn't become common knowledge, I thought.

Nonna greeted me in the old manner. "Ciao, gioia! How are you this morning? Always the early riser, I see."

"Ciao, Nonna! You know what they say? Chi dorme non prende pesce (he who sleeps does not catch fish)."

"Yes, indeed," she replied. Most of the time Nonna disliked my being unhappy and she appeared to have regard and trust in me. But of course, she had to uphold the precious Sicilian customs and traditions by making sure that nothing would taint my reputation. Being steeped in history and in the ancient ways, she was not aware that times were changing.

"Ciao, Marianna," said Carolina, swallowing a mouthful of coffee and milk. "I was looking for you this morning," she continued, "but you had already left when I woke up."

"Did you want something?" I inquired.

"No, I was just wondering if you have met many friends and whether you're enjoying the trip. I hardly ever see you. It's like when we were back home. You were always out. You were either at school, at Feo with Sara and Peppe, or some other part of the estate."

"Yes, I cherished the task of overseeing the workers and visiting the houses of the coloni and their families. I loved riding my horse and being in touch with nature," I replied with a sigh. "As far as our trip is concerned," I continued, "I am enjoying the experience and have made a few friends. There's one in particular I like very much," I said thinking of Lina and her sad story. "What about you, Carolina? Have you made friends?"

"Yes, I've met a few young people I like. Actually, I'm going to meet them now," said Carolina. She wiped her mouth with the napkin, and excusing herself, left.

"Carolina, be careful!" exclaimed Nonna.

"Be careful," echoed Mother.

There were only a few years difference in age between Carolina and me, yet she looked much younger than I did. Perhaps it was because I was considerably taller than she was. I think Carolina took after the paternal side of the family, in size that is. Turning to Mamma, I asked, "Where are you going after breakfast?"

"Perhaps in the sitting room to read a book or write some letters that we can post at the next port of call."

Mother looked somewhat despondent. Maybe she was having second thoughts about our intrepid adventure. She was not a secure person most of the time, but now what I was noticing was something much more than insecurity. Anxiety and fear were in her voice, that fear that had gripped her many times in the past.

"Are you sure you are all right, Marianna? You are not too unhappy about us going to Australia, are you? You know that if we don't like it once we arrive there, we can always come back." Her voice trembled in trying to swallow and conceal her tears, lest they should come flooding out and shatter her poised image. She looked defenseless. I wished she would cry and release all those repressed emotions. I felt the old compassion surfacing in my heart.

"I'm fine, Mamma, and as you said, we can always come back." Normally I would have repeated Carmela's perennial declaration that "No one ever returns from Australia," but I did not have the heart. She looked so lost and desolate. Something was suddenly worrying her. It was as if some hidden secret had surfaced from the depths of her being and she was feeling the pangs of a guilty conscience. But I know all Mother's secrets, I told myself. Yet, knowing my mother so well, I felt that there was something she had managed to mask and keep to herself. I must find out! I will have to make sure the two of us are alone and then ask her what it is she is hiding, I vowed to myself.

As we were leaving the breakfast table, once again Mother reiterated the same habitual warning.

"Be careful, Marianna, and don't socialize with strangers." She uttered the words without conviction—as if she did not care what I did. She seemed to have reverted to the past before the euphoria of leaving it behind. Mother had not realized that the past traveled with you no matter how far the journey.

There was no doubt about it! Mamma was apprehensive about something. Once she decided she was worried about some overstated and despairing notion, there was no way one could redirect her thinking toward a more cheerful and positive thought. She became fixated and fearful with some idea and there was no easy way to dissuade or thwart her from her preoccupation.

Soon I will ask mother what's worrying her, but not now. Today is such a beautiful day, and I don't want to spoil it, I thought to myself. I was hoping to see Guido and learn about the magnificent and breathtaking Red Sea, whose name, it seemed to me, was a misnomer.

When I went on deck, nearly everyone on board ship was at the rails gazing at the waters. Guido, taking advantage of the fact that everyone was intent on observing the blue Red Sea, came close to me, no doubt to give me the usual history and geography lesson. Since he had found out that I was an avid student for listening and learning, he took every opportunity to act as my teacher. After all, every good talker loves a keen listener. "Why is it called Red Sea when it's a glistering blue?" I asked pointing to the waters.

"It depends if you're a poet or a scientist," he said pensively.

"What do you mean?"

"The poet lauds its beauty at the setting of the sun. The reflection of the sunset makes the waters seem scarlet. I have seen the magnificence of the red-colored waters as the sun slowly descends behind the horizon. Its beauty is indeed inspiring." I could listen to Guido for hours on end. I could tell he was fascinated with the world he traveled.

"As a matter of fact, the same can be said of other seas. I suppose they all become tinged with red at sunset," I replied.

"I can see you want a more convincing explanation. Obviously, you are more of a scientist than a poet," said Guido, smiling. He was quite handsome when he smiled. His eyes seemed to light up.

"Why does a person have to be one or the other? Can't one be both a scientist and a poet?" I said thoughtfully.

"I suppose one can be both a scientist and a poet, Signorina Marianna. I actually had not given that much thought since everyone seems to think of them as opposites. According to popular opinion, the scientist deals in fact, and the poet uses his imagination to describe something."

"I don't think it is as clear cut as all that. I personally think one needs imagination to even describe a simple fact, otherwise the description, if one can call it that, is limited, bare, unclothed, and therefore uninteresting." Realizing that our discussion had digressed considerably, I asked, "But please Guido, tell me what the scientists are saying regarding the sea being called the Red Sea?"

"They say that it is either the red coral on the reef, or the planktonic algae. It seems these organisms leave a red scum on the edge of the water. So, I assume it can be one or all of those things: the sunset, the red coral, or the red scum left by the floating algae. No one knows for certain," said Guido shrugging his shoulders. Turning to look at me, he added, "What do you think? It seems that even the scientists are uncertain and therefore the subject is open to interpretations."

"In that case I prefer to believe both in the romantic vision of the poet and part of the scientific discovery. The different species of the coral could give the water a red reflection, even though at the moment, I see nothing but bright, sparkling blue. I refuse to believe, though, in the red scum left behind by the algae. The water looks too clean and too clear for it to be infested by algae," I said, trying to convince myself, for I could not tolerate the thought that scum could be polluting this paradise.

"The Red Sea," continued Guido, "is a submerged rift valley, 1,400 miles long and up to 225 miles wide. In parts it is over seven thousand feet deep. As you know, the Suez Canal joins it to the Mediterranean and the strait of Bab el Mandeb and the Gulf of Aden to the Indian Ocean. The sea is highly saline and rather warm."

"In a few days we will be navigating the Indian Ocean," I said with a shiver that did not go unnoticed by Guido.

"Are you feeling all right, Signorina Marianna?" asked Guido. There was concern in his voice.

"It's nothing. Just the thought of having to cross the Indian Ocean is rather scary and overwhelming. I've never traveled across an ocean before. And to myself I thought, Most certainly that will be the point of no return! Once again, I shivered.

"The Indian Ocean is not that much different from the seas we have traveled so far. Maybe just a little rougher in spots, that's all." Guido was unaware that he was making me a little nervous.

"Until now, we had nothing but magnificent weather, sunny skies, and calm seas. I suppose, we are bound to encounter a tempest or two in the Indian Ocean." I felt apprehensive.

"Are you going out, Marianna? Don't forget that today is Sunday, and we have to go to Mass. Don't go too far," said Mother dispassionately. Her unusual jubilation about going to Australia to meet her wayward and rambling father and her proper and self-righteous husband—namely, my father, seemed to have vanished. She was left with the reality of things, plus that something, which was resurfacing to haunt her. I could see the telltale signs of depression—the extreme gloom, the faraway look, the feeling of inadequacy, the inability to concentrate, anxiety and distress, and the incapacity to function properly.

All of these symptoms, if not yet intense, were present nevertheless. Soon the valerian drops would be needed, given that mother had brought the herbal medicine with her. I realized I had to find a few minutes alone with Mother to ask what the problem was. This might help avoid the incursion of the disorder, or at least minimize it. At first, she would resist talking to me but then she would find relief in sharing her dilemma. She always did; she turned to me for strength. She used to say I gave her courage.

At Mass, the chaplain read from the book of Genesis 12:1: "The Lord said to Abraham: 'Go forth from the land of your kinsfolk and from your father's house to the land that I will show you.'" He also read from the book of Exodus 14:15–17: "The Lord said to Moses … Tell the Israelites to go forward. And you lift up your staff and, with hand outstretched over the sea, split the sea in two, that the Israelites may pass through it on dry land."

It was obvious that the priest was equating Abraham to us, and the "Promised Land" to "Australia." I must admit, his concept was clever and appropriate. It was, in a sense, our Exodus, and the Red Sea was reminiscent of the Exodus of long ago. It was here that the miraculous deliverance of the Israelites by God, through Moses, who led them across the Red Sea to Mount Sinai, had occurred.

After Mass, I went on deck. Looking at the sea, I wondered whether God would make of us "a great nation." Whether He would make our "name great," so that we would "be a blessing" to others. He would say, "I will bless those who bless you and curse those who curse you. All the communities of the earth shall find blessing in you" (Exodus 12:2–3). I smiled at my pretentiousness and at my weird sense of humor. We are hardly the chosen people, I thought to myself. After all, unlike Abraham, we have left our sheep, our cows, and our mules behind, and our belongings, depending on our social status, fit in a trunk or our suitcases.

And so we sailed on the spectacular Red Sea, Saudi Arabia on one side and Egypt, Sudan, and Ethiopia on the other. We were traveling toward our next port of call, Port Aden in southern Yemen.

5

PORT ADEN

As the sun gradually descended beyond the horizon, the vision of the poet came to life; a vision of what appeared to be an exquisite depiction painted by the master painter Himself. The sunset was radiating the water, coloring it with dramatic hues. At first there was a tinge of red. And then the different shades of scarlet beauty burst forth and filled the twilight, giving it an aura of ancient mystery. Perhaps both the sun and the corals on the reef drew from one another to produce such splendor.

"The Red Sea," I whispered in wonder, "isn't a misnomer after all." The Red Sea was a crimson red. What a wondrous miracle! I thought in awe of the transformation, which took place before my very eyes.

I was in meditative contemplation when I felt a powerful presence next to me. As I was abruptly interrupted, I jumped. I felt I had been torn away from a precious moment, which could not be recaptured again, at least not in my lifetime.

"Buona sera, Signorina. Sorry, I didn't mean to startle you," said the young man politely.

"You didn't startle me," I lied.

"Please permit me to introduce myself; my name is Roberto," he said with a smile.

I was a little angry and I wished Roberto were on the other side of the ship looking in another direction. I wished he would leave me alone to contemplate this aesthetically awesome scenery, which for centuries had captured the imagination of poets and lovers, not to mention the biblical significance of this place. Reluctantly, I turned toward Roberto and coldly replied, "Piacere Roberto, my name is Marianna."

"I've noticed you before, but you're always surrounded by people, and I wasn't able to talk to you, Signorina Marianna." Roberto sounded resolute and spoke without hesitation. I had also noticed him stare at me, but I wasn't about to tell him in case it would inflate his ego and he would think I fancied him or something outrageous like that.

"I was wondering if you would like to go out with me tonight," said Roberto with a hint of self-assurance.

"Out where? I think we are already out, don't you? Actually, we could not be more out than this," I said, pointing at the wide-open sea. As soon as I said that I realized I had been a little discourteous. To soften the sharp edge and the somewhat sarcastic words, I forced a smile. Soon, though, I understood my smiling was a mistake, for he appeared encouraged. Roberto looked at me and said seriously, "Not only are you beautiful, Signorina Marianna, but you also have a sense of humor."

I could not believe it. This chap had not realized that I was irritated by his interruption, which prevented me from admiring the most astonishing vista I was not likely to see ever again in my life. Furthermore, he mistook annoyance for humor. "What a dunce," I mumbled under my breath.

"You haven't answered my question," Roberto persisted, a hint of arrogance in his voice.

"What question was that?"

"Will you go out with me?"

What an imbecile! I thought to myself, and aloud I said, "I thought I had."

"No, you haven't. You haven't given me a direct answer. I believe," continued Roberto, "they're showing a good film this evening, I hope you can join me."

This chap doesn't understand subtlety, so I had better be blunt if I want to get rid of him, I thought to myself. I said, "I am sorry I can't go to see the film with you. I've promised a friend I would go with her."

"Oh! You are going out with a female friend? Then we could go as a group, can't we?"

I am done with being courteous! The time has come to make him realize he is being a nuisance. This chap reminds me of Tano, I said to myself.

The thought of the forceful Tano and the near-miss tragedy made me shiver. Thankfully, my dear friend Peppe had saved me from Tano's lewd advance. The incident, which I thought had been locked away within me for good, was resurfacing.

I resented Roberto for being the cause of my recollections, which renewed the hurt and humiliation I had felt, and which brought me back to a time I wanted to desperately forget. I realized Roberto was staring at me waiting for an answer.

"No, thank you, I don't go out with strangers." This time I was purposely sharp. I wanted him to finally comprehend that I wasn't interested. Roberto looked angry. In the realization that there was a person that did not think he was the center of the universe, his enormous ego was shattered.

"You Sicilians are very insular and not up with the times. In northern Italy, where I come from, we are outgoing and sociable," said Roberto, overtly irritated at my refusal. Since my denial was inconceivable to him, he decided that the fault must be mine. He had no idea that his inflated narcissistic ego and pretentious personality repelled me.

"Since I come from an island, I make no excuses for being 'insular,' as you put it; nor do I make excuses for not being 'up with the times,' as I feel that's not always the best thing." I could not believe what I was saying. I had always maintained that my family was too insular, too traditional, and did not move with the times, and now I was defending what I had tried to reject.

I was angry because Roberto was protracting the age-old hostility of north versus south. However, he had chosen the wrong person to exhibit his sense of superiority. What made the northerners think they were superior, anyway? "The need for supremacy is born out of insecurity." Without realizing it, I had spoken those words out loud. As I walked away, Roberto looked perplexed.

I went to see the film with Lina and a group of young people. In the distance I saw Roberto all alone. I looked away. I did not want to anger him any further because I felt he was the kind of person who would take revenge. People like him did not just come from the north or the south, they were found slithering away in every zone of any given country and even on board ship. I shivered at the thought.

I remembered Sara's words back at Feo: "Always trust your instincts; they will never let you down." I had promised I would, so trusting my every instinct, I vowed not to cross Roberto's path, at least not while I was alone.

The next morning, everyone was running backward and forward. It could only mean that we had reached Port Aden. And so, it was. I looked around for Guido for my usual lesson, but he was far too busy. No doubt I would meet him later. He would not back out on his role of tutor—he enjoyed it too much, as I enjoyed being tutored.

"Beautiful, isn't it?" Guido, discharging himself temporarily from his duties, ran toward me.

"It's a totally different world than the one I have known up to now," I replied pensively.

"Yes, indeed, it is a different world," asserted Guido.

"Tell me about it. Tell me about Port Aden."

"Port Aden is the commercial capital of Yemen. It is situated at the southwest corner of the Arabian Peninsula, and it has traded since ancient times, about three thousand years, I think. It is one of the largest natural harbors. "Halfway between Europe and the Far East, Aden is located on a major world trading route through the Suez Canal," continued Guido.

"I believe our Venetian merchant, Marco Polo, and the Arab traveler Ibn Batula, who wrote an account of his travels titled the Rihlah, visited Aden," I said. I wanted to show that I also had some knowledge of Yemen. It was a newly acquired knowledge meant to impress Guido. I think he guessed, though, that my whit of information came from one of the ship's library books.

"Yes. Indeed. They visited Aden in the eleventh and twelfth centuries," added Guido with a smile.

Suddenly something else caught my attention. I noticed a ship docked some distance away from ours. It wasn't anything like the one we were traveling on. The Australia was brand new and sparkled in the sun, while the other ship, in comparison, looked battered and old. It obviously had seen better days, yet I felt that my destiny was somehow tied with the old, run-down boat.

I was astonished at my own thoughts. Was I having a premonition? Was I becoming one of those Sicilians who could leap forward into the future and know what was in store for them and their loved ones? I wanted nothing to do with premonitions and presentiments. I wanted nothing to do with the knowledge of what tomorrow might bring. I wanted to have the ability and the freedom to shape my tomorrows. I wanted to live my life with optimism and hopeful expectancy and not with the continuous apprehension of a dismal destiny that was lurking in the dark corners of the mind, ready to strike and possess the very soul when it was least expected. I even wanted to choose my own thoughts—happy thoughts, which, I felt, had the potential of creating objective realities.

I thought of my great-grandmother, Grazia, who had been brought up to believe that gazing at the stars would give her warts. So, with the exception of a few happy years, her life was marred with the fear that some tragedy was furtively waiting to assault her and demand retribution, and unavoidably it did do just that. What an existence! Always crowded with constant torturous mental anguish. I, on the other hand, would gaze at the infinity and magnitude of the universe, at the myriad of celestial objects, which radiated light and energy.

How magnificent those points of light were on a clear night, especially at sea. The luminous and resplendent sky, reflected in the waters, gave the feeling of being encompassed and cradled by the creator Himself.

Perceptibly, one realized being a part of the whole creation, even if an infinitesimal part. Yet that tiny part was needed to make the universe complete. Every one of us had a purpose in life and we had the potential and the choice to either fulfill that purpose or squander it. I would live each day with the anticipation that zillions of wondrous possibilities could unfold, possibilities that had to be seized or else they would be lost forever. I would accept the challenges life had to offer. Contrary to my great-grandmother, I would gaze at the stars, hoping to be sprinkled with the auspicious stardust.

What an uproarious brain I had, it kept on chattering and bouncing from one subject to another incessantly. It resembled a group of monkeys making repetitive noises and jumping from tree to tree in a jungle, I thought to myself, smiling.

Unquestionably, though, the feeling that something was about to happen to change my life forever kept on surfacing. Undoubtedly, I was having one of those Sicilian premonitions. I was being forewarned about some future event, but it did not seem an imminent disastrous event, as it usually was with Sicilian premonitions—hence it was not a Sicilian premonition at all.

Maybe it was a prediction—a kind of prophecy in which the information was obtained through a psychic gift, a divine inspiration, by reading the signs, or by the altering of consciousness. But since there was no prophecy, just a feeling that one may have after a considerable amount of alcohol consumption, one could hardly call it a "prediction" in the true sense of the word. But I had not consumed any alcohol, and the crazy feeling persisted. I hiccupped, I trembled, I shivered, and all the follicles in my body were alerted to the imminent whatever, as I kept on looking at the old ship.

"Signorina Marianna. Baronessina Marianna." Guido's voice seemed to come from another planet.

He has found out about this baronessina thing. I wasn't aware he knew. I was a little annoyed.

"My name is Marianna." I was a little abrupt.

"I am not permitted to talk to a passenger in a familiar way," replied Guido.

"Why not?"

"It's policy."

Guido changed the subject by asking a question: "Why are you fascinated with the Hellenic Prince? You've been staring at it for some time."

"What's the name of the boat?" I asked. There was a sense of urgency in my voice.

"The Hellenic Prince. You can barely see the name," said Guido pointing to the flank of the ship.

"Is it Greek?"

"It is now. It was an English warship, but the Greeks bought it, and now it is used as a passenger ship. But why are you so interested in it?" Guido appeared baffled that my interest had been diverted from his tutoring abilities to a rickety, ancient boat.

"I don't know." I was puzzled myself.

"Are you going down to visit Aden?" asked Guido.

"I doubt it. My mother and grandmother would lock me away if they could. They are always scared of my being abducted."

"They're looking out for you."

"Sure."

"It might be just as well since the passengers of the Hellenic Prince have been given the permission to visit the Australia. It appears we are going to have quite a few visitors today," stated Guido.

I didn't know why the news should make me happy, but it did.

"When … when are they coming on board?" I asked anxiously.

"Most of them after lunch, although, some passengers, out of courtesy, without a doubt will be invited to lunch with the captain," replied Guido.

I must have an early lunch and be on deck when the passengers arrive, I thought.

When Nonna, Mamma, and Carolina came into the dining room, to their amazement, I was already sitting at the table. Usually, in trying to avoid my family, I was the last to arrive and the first to leave. Today, however, I wanted to gulp down my food quickly in order not to miss whatever it was that was pulling me toward the passengers of the Hellenic Prince. Deep in thought, I jumped when Nonna spoke to me.

"You seemed miles away, Marianna. What were you thinking?"

"Oh! Nothing."

"Why are you here so early?" asked mother. I shrugged my shoulders, fully aware that my mother had little interest in my reply.

Food took ages to come; no doubt, the stewards were too busy serving the guests from the Hellenic Prince. Halfway through our lunch, excusing myself, and before anyone had a chance to say anything, I got up from the table quickly and left. I could see the astonished look in my family's eyes. As I reached the deck, a sense of expectancy and suspense overtook me. It was as if the rest of my life depended on this moment.

I looked around and saw crowds of people approaching the companionway. I kept on staring at their faces as they climbed the stairs, not knowing exactly what or who I was looking for. I felt a little disillusioned because all those faces meant nothing to me. There was no one who stood out in the crowd that remotely interested me. They were the usual throng that shoved and pushed to go nowhere. I was just about to go, yet something had me nailed to the floor. People brushed past me, and the odd imbecile emitted the so-called wolf whistle. Idiots like that annoyed and bored me to tears. I had no time for them and took no notice of them. How long had I stood there? I had no idea. Was it a few hours or a lifetime?

I think I will go to my cabin, I told myself, feelings have nothing to do with reality. A while back I had felt elated and in suspense, now the feeling of anticipation had turned into a kind of doleful and glum mood.

I turned to go when a voice brought me to a halt.

"Michael, what are you staring at? Are you coming or are you going to stand there? Hurry, we must go."

I suddenly saw him. He was looking at me, and as our eyes met, I fell in love for life. No question! He was the love of my life. In that very instant I knew that if I didn't marry him, I would not marry anyone else. I was sure he felt the same way for his friend had to pull him by the arm to try to drag him away. He kept on resisting the pull. He did not want to go away, and I did not want him to go away. I wanted to talk to him, to ask him if we could meet again. I knew his name was Michael but what was his surname? How could

I find him? Where was he going? He pulled away from his friend and came toward me.

"My name is Michael. What is yours?" he asked with urgency.

"Marianna," I replied.

"Where are you going?"

"Australia."

"Michael we must really go," interrupted his friend, "the ship will sail soon."

"I will find you!" he said to me. There was a tone of despair in his voice.

"I will be waiting."

He touched my hand, and I trembled. I felt I was living a lifetime in an instant. Then, as suddenly as he had appeared, he disappeared from my life. His friend had pulled him away from me. I felt devastated. What an idiot I was! I had told him I was going to Australia as if Australia was a small town instead of a huge continent.

He could ask the captain my forwarding address. No! The captain would not disclose such private information. Anyway, our ship was leaving port soon. Once again, my heart was wrenched as the crew worked to weigh anchor. The ship started to move, and this time I was leaving behind the rest of my life, for life without Michael was not worth living. He was the person I had dreamed about and was certain I would meet one day. Now that I had met him, he was probably traveling in a different direction than me. The so-called "destiny" was indeed cruel. It gives a hint of happiness to then take it away.

I kept on looking at the void that the ship was creating, both internally and externally, when Guido approached me.

"You look so gloomy and distressed!" he exclaimed.

"I don't want to talk about it," I replied sharply. Guido looked perplexed at my harsh response.

"What could have happened in such a short time to change your mood so drastically?"

"Life can be so cruel." I hoped Guido would leave me alone. I had no intention of listening to his relentless chatter, and I was in no mood for lectures.

"So cynical for someone so young," said Guido with a sigh.

6

THE INDIAN OCEAN

I was having a wonderful dream; Michael's gentle eyes were looking into mine. He was holding my hand, and we were planning our future together. We were so happy! We were meant to be together. "When we say our marriage vows in front of the priest and pronounce the words, 'until death do us part,'" I whispered to Michael, "I don't think I want us to limit our marriage to our death. I want us to be married for all eternity."

Michael nodded and replied, "Exactly what I was thinking. Since the beginning of time, we were meant to be together, so it stands to reason that we should be married until the end of time."

"It's settled then! We shall ask the priest if it's possible for the words to be altered a little. We will tell him that we do not wish to say the words that we should be parted at death, but instead we want to be married for all eternity."

"It's settled!" replied Michael.

Loud noises awoke me. At first, I did not know where I was. The dream seemed so real that I thought I was in another place and in another time. I was so disappointed to once again be wrenched away from Michael and to realize that something that was only a dream could appear so vividly true. I was on the same huge boat traveling to Australia. Probably Michael was traveling on another route. Will I see him again? Will my dream come true? I asked myself, feeling sad. In my heart, I felt that somewhere, sometime, I would come face-to-face with Michael, and our meeting would have an end.

The huge ship was swaying from side to side. The top deck almost touched the water, and the enormous waves came crashing across the ship. I had never seen anything so terrifying before. The Indian Ocean was greeting us with violent rage. I had heard or read somewhere that the Indian Ocean's climate north of the equator was strongly influenced by monsoons. Apparently, from October to April, strong northern winds blow. From May to September south and west winds are prominent. The Indian Ocean, Guido would say, is the third largest body of water in the world, and normally, I would be attentive and listen to his every word. However, at the moment, I did not feel like listening to anything anyone had to say.

Furthermore, both passengers and crew were nowhere to be seen; the whole ship seemed deserted. Because of the wild weather, everyone had withdrawn to the safety of their cabins. I felt enclosed and alone; I wanted to talk to someone about Michael, but with whom would I share my story? Mother was worried about something, and, it seemed to me, that the closer we got to Australia, the gloomier and more self-absorbed she became.

I would have loved to talk to her about Michael, but in the mood she was in, she would not hear what I had to say, let alone be interested. On the other hand, I should ask what was worrying her, but I also was not able to listen, much less care. Deep down, I did care, though, and one of these days I would broach the subject of what was the cause of her sullen mood.

Not knowing what to do with myself, swaying and tossing from side to side of the corridor, I made my way toward the library. The ship was still deserted and so was the library. I picked up a book on the Indian Ocean and indolently opened it up at random. The page showed a map, which surrounded the ocean. Suddenly, as I usually was around books, I became interested. The book made much more sense now that I was somewhere in the ocean. For the first time, I realized the magnitude of such a body of water. The Indian Ocean in the north is bordered by southern Asia, in the west by the Arabian Peninsula and Africa; in the east by the Malay Peninsula, the Sunda Islands, and Australia; and in the south by the Southern Ocean.

We were traveling fast; the stormy weather condition had momentarily subsided. Occasionally, I went toward the stern of the boat to admire the different kinds of fish jumping out of the water. The huge whales, in particular, fascinated me. The ship kept on slicing through the water, and I wondered how far this land called Australia was. Deep in thought, the voice of the person who had crept beside me without my notice greeted me. It was Guido, I felt remorseful for having been sharp toward him, but he obviously understood my sadness, for he said, "Feeling better now?"

"I'm sorry for having been rude, you didn't deserve it. You've been a good friend to me. There was no reason to take my frustration out on you."

"No need to apologize! What are friends for? If not to understand when a friend is in distress? Now that you're in a better mood, may I ask what was the matter with you?" asked Guido, hesitantly.

"I prefer not to talk about it just yet. Maybe later." And changing the subject, I said, "Some storm we had."

"The Indian Ocean is notorious for storms. Depending on the time of the year, tropical storms can be dangerous in this area. Not for us, though!" he added quickly in case his declaration had frightened me. It actually did a little. Remembering the storm of the past few days and that the ship was tossed from side to side, I had no problem in believing that even our huge vessel could be easily catapulted. With my vivid imagination I saw the scene and shuddered. Unaware of my anxiety, Guido stated: "We're nearing Colombo."

7

Colombo, Ceylon

The morning that we arrived at Colombo, I was filled with hopeful expectation. Maybe the Hellenic Prince would arrive at the same time. Deep down, I did not think it would happen. The boat on which Michael was sailing could not match the speed of the Australia, but then, being smaller, it might have the velocity.

As usual, I was deluding myself. I did not even know in which direction the Hellenic Prince was sailing. We stayed at the port of Colombo from dawn to dusk, and as usual Guido came and stood next to me.

"Judging from the scenery, I imagine, Colombo must be a fabulous place with beautiful palaces, wonderful temples, and churches." Since I already knew that Guido would start talking about the island soon, I spoke first.

"Yes, it is a magnificent place rich in ancient culture. Did you know that Ceylon is an island shaped like an enormous tear?"

"No, I didn't," I replied, a little distracted.

"Only thirty-one miles separates Ceylon from India. The island is situated in the center of the Indian Ocean, a precarious place."

"It's very beautiful." I said, looking around the port of Colombo.

I could see that Guido followed my gaze. He said, "The port of Colombo is one of the largest artificial ports of the world."

"Is it really?"

"Yes, it is! But you are not listening. Your interest seems to be elsewhere. What are you looking at, Marianna?"

It was the first time Guido had called me by my first name. "Oh, nothing in particular, just interested in the other boats around the port."

"You wouldn't be looking for the Hellenic Prince by any chance, would you? And if you are why on earth for? I haven't been able to understand the reason."

"It's nothing, I was just wondering where she was traveling to. I saw many people who came on our ship and was speculating on where their destination might be."

"Most probably Australia," said Guido thoughtfully.

My heart skipped a beat. I can find Michael in Australia. I felt hopeful. But then coming back to my senses, but Australia is a huge continent! I said to myself, feeling a sense of melancholy.

"Animal life is copious in Ceylon," continued Guido, with determination to achieve what he had intended to. "Of course, first and foremost there are the elephants, leopards, deer, monkeys, sloth bears, wild boar, cobras, crocodiles, dugong, and turtles, not to mention the different kinds of birds."

"Did you say cobras?"

"Yes, I did!"

"I'm terrified of snakes. I wouldn't like coming face to face with a cobra."

"Not many people would," said Guido with a smile.

"If it weren't for the monsoons and the snakes, this place would be a paradise, but then every paradise has its snake."

"Indeed! As I was saying, the monsoons are rather terrifying also. Ceylon is subjected to two monsoons at different parts of the island. In the Yala season from May to August, the southwest monsoon brings heavy falls of rain to the southern, western, and central regions. From October to January, the Maha season, the northeast monsoon brings rain to the north and east of the island."

"Guido, you really have a great knowledge about these places. I'm impressed!"

"It's nothing. It's information I pick up in my travels."

Guido excused himself because he had to go to work, and once again I was left alone with my thoughts. From a distance I saw Lina and realized I had not seen her in a few days. The weather had prevented us from meeting one another.

"Ciao, Lina! How are you?"

"Ciao, Marianna! Well thanks! We had some bad weather. I didn't think this huge ship could be shaken, but I was wrong. It shook like crazy. I have never seen anything like that in the Mediterranean."

"No, not quite. But, at times I have seen ships appear and disappear in the waves of the sea."

"Yes, you're right, there have been times when the storms toss ships around, but the storms of the Mediterranean cannot be compared with the monsoons of the Indian Ocean."

Lina and I chattered for a while and then parted. People from Colombo started to come on board to visit the Australia. An elegant looking official came toward me; apparently, he had been watching me and liked what he saw. When he approached me, I thought he wanted to ask for directions, but to my surprise he asked me to go with him: he wanted me to be his wife. I said I could not possibly go with him since I was going to Australia to meet my father. That, however, did not deter him from insisting that I should go with him. When I declined the request, I could see that my denial had made him angry. He then placed him arm next to mine to compare the color of our skin.

"Is this the reason why you won't come with me?" he said.

"No! Color of the skin has nothing to do with it. I don't even know you! How could I possibly come with you?" I could see that he was growing angrier by the minute, and I was becoming more frightened by the second.

He was pulling my arm, and he was hurting me. With much relief, I saw a group of people coming toward us, including a few members of the crew. Quietly but firmly, he was ushered off the boat. For the rest of the day, however, no matter where I went, I had escorts, one on each side of me. I felt so embarrassed being escorted, though no doubt that was exactly what Mamma and Nonna wanted.

The sunset was extremely beautiful; suddenly, it was dusk. We would be going soon. Actually, as I looked down, I saw that the ship had already been disengaged from the port. Surely, my bodyguards would leave me alone now? I asked myself. They did not do so until we were on the high seas.

Before darkness descended upon us, I looked back and saw a boat following us. "The Hellenic Prince," I whispered, my heart filled with joy. For a long stretch, I saw the lights of the boat behind us. Then, the lights became smaller and smaller, and dimmer and dimmer until they could not be seen anymore. Michael was so near, yet so far. I felt such a sense of loss. I did not know when, I did not know in which corner of the continent, but one day Michael and I would meet face-to-face. On that day, I would have to somehow convince my father that Michael was the man for the rest of my life and beyond.

"Please God, let it be so." I prayed with all my heart.

8

THE EQUATOR

We were well and truly beyond the Pillars of Hercules. We had more than reached the point of no return. It was Australia for the rest of my life. I would never see my island again. I had not realized before now how much influence Carmela had on my way of thinking. The mythological Pillars of Hercules had nothing to do with our route, yet I could not take out of my mind the idea that we had reached a point of no return. We had been on the ship for so long and we traveled so far that going back seemed an enormous impossibility.

The land of Australia was at the end of the world, and our trip was an adventure beyond comprehension. We had left everything that we knew and loved for the great unknown. God only knew what sacrifices and hardships awaited us.

Everywhere there was an atmosphere of excitement and festivities, as people were getting ready to party for the crossing of the equator. Another mythological creature was awaiting us: King Neptune apparently was in charge of the equator and had to be appeased in order to give his permission for us to cross it. These people were as delusional as my mother and grandmother; they acted as if this trip were a pleasure cruise, not going to Australia to work. I guess, though, it was better to take life with good humor rather than wallow in misery.

The costumes for the party looked very impressive. The weather was extremely hot, and the swimming pool was crowded. Suddenly, someone dressed as King Neptune, with his trident and all, appeared. Delicious food and drink were offered to him, and the ladies dressed in colorful costumes danced, then they were offered as a sacrifice to him by being thrown in the pool. King Neptune's anger was abated with all the folderol, and the permission for us to cross the equator was granted.

The next stop—Australia! However, before that happened, I had to talk to mother to find out what was upsetting her. Determined to discover her problem, I went to look for her. I found Mother sitting in the lounge reading but judging by her faraway look, her concentration was elsewhere.

"Mamma, what are you thinking? What's worrying you?" Mother jumped at the sound of my voice and reluctantly was brought to the present.

"Oh! Nothing," she mumbled.

"There must be something wrong. You look so troubled. What could have happened to take away the happiness you felt to go to Australia to be with Papà and to reconcile with your father?"

"This is just it! It isn't going to happen anymore. It was a dream, a foolish dream. Too good to be true." Mamma looked disheartened and despondent.

"What is it that it isn't going to happen? Mamma, please tell me! You are making me nervous."

"You know I had a dream to reunite the family, but now it is all impossible."

"What's impossible?" Something happened to Papà?" Mother hesitated before answering, and she looked absent and dazed.

"No, nothing has happened to you father—not the way you think, anyway.

"What is it then? you're making me frantic. You'd better start at the beginning and tell me what's bothering you before I have a fit. I have a right to know."

"I suppose you have," said Mother, slouching on the sofa. She looked exhausted.

"You remember that your father went to Queensland and then decided to settle in Western Australia?"

"Yes, I remember."

"He had relatives in Queensland, but I wanted him to go to Western Australia when through the Italian consulate I found out the whereabouts of my father. After so many years that my father lived in Australia, without so much as writing a single letter to his wife or to his own daughter, I decided that I wanted him in my life."

"I never understood that. I never understood why you would think that he could settle down to family life after so many years. What were you, twelve years old when he left? And now look at you —you're a grown woman with two daughters!"

"Yes, you're right, Marianna, but I wanted so much to be reunited. I wanted Nonna to have her husband back."

"I thought Papà had met up with him."

"Yes, he has. And at first my father seemed anxious to see us. He even sent a proxy for us to sell the property his parents left him. He also signed the documents for Nonna to come to Australia."

"And then?"

"Then he changed his mind. Apparently, the husband of one of his lovers died and she went to live with him. Your father told him she could not stay with him because his wife was coming soon. He then wanted to cancel the documents so she would have no way of migrating. Papà was worried that if he would succeed in doing so, I would not come to Australia either because I would not leave my mother alone."

"So, your father does not know that we are coming?"

"No, he doesn't."

"What about Nonna? Does she know all of this?"

"No, she doesn't."

"What a mess! I exclaimed.

"How come you didn't tell Nonna?"

"Because she would not come with us."

I was dumbfounded. So much machination! "What a mess! What a sordid mess," I kept on repeating. Turning to Mother, I asked, "Does your father still work in the Kalgoorlie gold mines?"

"No, he has retired from the mines. He now works on his farm. Your father mentioned that he grows vegetables, tomatoes for tomato sauce especially."

"And this lady lives on the farm with him?"

"Yes."

"From what I know, Mamma, your father hasn't changed much. If anything, he has changed for the worse."

"What am I to do?" cried mother.

"You must tell Nonna, and after that I wouldn't know. We cannot go back now. When we arrive in Australia, Papà will decide what to do, no doubt."

9

AUSTRALIA

The rest of the voyage was uneventful. The weather was mild. The Indian Ocean had calmed down somewhat and was just ripples and waves that appeared to be pushing us toward the land of Australia. In the last few days, drizzling rain kept on coming down.

Everyone was suddenly quiet; the euphoria of the past days was gone. People were introspective; the reality of what was about to happen had sunk in. The silent rain resembled their soundless tears. Their eyes were dry; only their hearts sobbed. The general question that no one had the courage to ask was, "What is awaiting us?"

We were unanimously scared. We had so little because we had left so much behind. We had left everything: our country, our relatives, and our friends. We had so much to do to recover at least part of our lives. We knew so little about the country where we were going to live from now on; we knew practically nothing about the people we were going to meet. Were they hospitable to foreigners? Of course, they would be. We weren't savages; we may be different, but we were the same race—all human beings. If the situation were reversed, we would welcome people from another land into our country—we always had.

People were hugging their cardboard suitcases in case that they too would be taken away from them. Who could blame them? The contents of those battered cases were all they had. I looked at all the people and, as if I was seeing them for the first time, I was proud of them. Most of them were sacrificing themselves for the love of their families. Some of them might not be high on the scale of literacy, but over the years, they had collected so much wisdom from the different cultures that had populated our land. Oh! How much respect I had for each one of them—my country people—my paesani.

Someone shouted: "Land! Land! Come quickly, we have arrived in Australia." That must be Fremantle out there. Some of us had indeed arrived; others had still a long way to go—Adelaide, Melbourne, Sydney, and Brisbane. Each one of us had a mission to accomplish, a life to give up. We said goodbye to the friends we had made. I hugged Lina and wished her good luck in her new marriage. She did the same to me; she wished I would find a good person whom I could share my life with. We also thanked the members of the crew we had been close to. Guido invited me to visit the ship on the next trip to Australia. I said I would if I lived close to Fremantle.

"Guido, I am so grateful for the lessons. I thank you so much."

"It was my pleasure; you are a very receptive pupil." I laughed while tears ran down my face.

"Cheer up, Marianna, you'll be meeting your father soon. And the Hellenic Prince should be here eventually," said Guido with a smile. "I do not know whether she'll be stopping in Fremantle, though," he continued. I felt myself blushing because I realized that he had guessed that my heart was on that raggedy old boat.

From on top of the ship Carolina had spotted Papà. "Look Marianna, there's Papà." I saw him also; he waved and blew kisses. I told Mamma that Papà was waiting for us, and for the first time in ages she was smiling. Finally, after what seemed a long time, we were allowed to disembark. I went to reach out to embrace my father, and I was stopped. I realized that we had been fenced off. We were then pushed away from the people who were waiting for us. I could not understand the separation, and I was shocked at the rudeness of the people. What had we done to deserve such hostility? To my enormous mortification, I would understand a little later.

10

HUMILIATION

I had predicted that migrants were seen as socially second-class citizens, but I had not anticipated that suddenly we were the lowest on the social scale. I wanted to go back home where we would be treated with respect. I had not asked for this. I was an innocent victim of migration. Actually, there were many innocent victims, if not all of us. Victims of something or other; victims of war; victims of poverty; victims of one's own pride like my father, and victims of one's own stupidity like my grandfather. Regardless of the reason, we were in the same boat, so to speak. Some people had promised their family that they would be away for a couple of years, but I saw that was a mammoth impossibility.

We were told not to touch the suitcases because they had to be inspected. We were then pushed and shoved toward a bus waiting for us. I did not understand why we were supposed to go on the bus, especially when we did not even know its destination. We could not even embrace our loved ones who came to meet us and had remained at the port of Fremantle. No one had told us anything. We simply obeyed orders because the men in charge looked pretty grim.

We may not have understood English, but we most assuredly understood the signs. No one uttered a word. Suddenly it was relatively dark, and the only thing that was visible was a rather barren countryside, miles and miles of flat brown land. We finally arrived at a place that looked like a camp. We all stared at each other and lifted our shoulders, which meant, "I don't know." When we came out of the bus, a group of people gathered and were talking. They were told rudely not to stay in groups and not to speak that "lingo." From now on we should speak English.

We entered the building; we were guided toward bathtubs separated by curtains. In each bathtub there was a murky brown liquid. We were told to undress and wash ourselves in that water. Suddenly it dawned on me that we were being disinfected. I was repulsed and tried to back out, but a big woman in some sort of uniform tried to pull my clothes off and pushed me toward the bathtub.

Maybe there was an epidemic of some sort, I told myself, but I had no knowledge of it. Furthermore, we were screened thoroughly before we left Italy. Of course, we could have picked up something on the way, but there was no reason to treat us like criminals of war. The smell of the fumigation of our clothes added insult to injury. We had to obey, though, or suffer the consequences, and judging by the appearance of these people, I dreaded what that would bring.

On the return trip to the wharf's big shed, everyone was silent. Our future as Australian immigrants appeared bleak indeed. Our arrival back in Fremantle's port was even more shattering than our bathing experience. All the suitcases had been forced open and their contents thrown on the ground. People were trying desperately to identify their possessions to put them back in their suitcases. Eventually those who had relatives waiting were able to run to them for a well-earned hug.

We, the Del Feo family were finally together. The first question I asked my father was, "Papà, when are we going back home?"

Papà looked sad and replied, "One day, but first we must give Australia a chance."

"I have nothing against Australia, I do not even know it to form an opinion. The people, however, do not seem to like us, at least the ones that I met. If this is a general feeling, then how can we survive?"

"Don't you worry! We shall survive, you wait until you make new friends. Things will appear different," said Father pensively.

We spent that night at a hotel in Fremantle. It was a Friday night and many people had been drinking and were drunk. They looked at us and shouted a word I did not understand, but father obviously did because he took Carolina and me by the hand and rushed us past the people into the foyer of the hotel. The following morning, we had to catch a plane to a town north of Fremantle.

Early the following morning we took a taxi that would take us to Perth's domestic airport to catch the plane toward the northwest, where my grandfather lived and where my father had rented a house for us. Maybe the people of this town will be different, I hoped. Our entrance and the first impressions of Australia was an unfortunate, humiliating, and demeaning experience that deep down I knew would last a lifetime. We were and always would be aliens. I felt wounded and unable to explain why I should be made to feel that way. So young to have every hope and dream shattered!

11

Toward Northwestern Australia

On the plane to our destination, my mother and father were having a very serious and involved conversation. No doubt they were discussing the situation that Nonna had to face on her arrival in the town where her husband was living. "Poor Donna Camilla, what had they done to her?" Carolina and I, even though wounded, were young and we would survive somehow, but what about Nonna and Mamma? Once the euphoria of meeting her husband was gone, and she had to deal with being laughed at and being ridiculed, what would she do? She was such a beautiful woman, but so emotionally fragile.

Looking out of the window of the plane one could see acres and acres of flat land that went on without end. So much land for such a small population! Suddenly I realized that the main reason that we were brought to Australia was to procreate and multiply to populate the land. After a while Papà came and sat in the seat behind Carolina and me. We could see that he had something on his mind and wanted to talk about it to us. He started:

"When we arrive at our home, we have to be very careful."

"Careful with what?" I replied sharply, for I guessed what was coming next.

"Careful in the way we talk and walk and the way we dress." Papà hesitated, then continued. "You know how we Italians tend to speak a little loud and express ourselves with our hands? Well, we can't do that anymore."

"Why not?" replied Carolina, taking the words out of my mouth.

"Because it's not done here," said Papà, who was finding this discussion progressively more difficult.

"Who says that?" I was close to being furious.

"The government, and the Australian people support the idea."

"So, the government makes the immigrants prisoners?" By now I had reached furious.

"You exaggerate, Marianna."

"I can't see it's an exaggeration when we can't talk the way we like, dress the way we like, and speak in our own language. Shouldn't we at least learn English first, before we are asked to speak it? And when you found out all of this, why didn't you return to your own country?"

"I wanted to give Australia a chance before I returned home."

By now I had put aside the Sicilian dictum of "Do not speak to your father like that" and was ready to yell at him, but a scene was avoided when the hostess signaled us to put on our seat belts because we were landing, and Father had to return to his seat.

At the airport, we caught a bus to town. The countryside appeared slightly different; there were lots of tomatoes growing. I saw Papà whisper something in mother's ear and point out to a farmhouse surrounded by tomato plants. I understood that my grandfather lived there. He was at the bottom of all of this; he was partly the reason why we had come to Australia.

We arrived at the home that my father had prepared for us—if one could call it home. It was a two-room house with a common bathroom and kitchen, which we were sharing with another Italian family with four children. It was all so ludicrous, and everything had an aura of an outlandish nightmare.

Papà looked a little embarrassed. It was obvious he was going to tell Nonna that her wayward husband had not changed since he had left Sicily in 1925. If anything, with age, instead of mellowing, he had become more predatory. He had an insatiable and voracious lust for low-life women.

"I really do not care for him; it's so long since we have been apart that I didn't even entertain the thought of living with him," said Nonna. "However, I should have been told before we left Italy. Had I known, I could have made different choices."

"You know that you're always welcome to stay with us?" replied Papà.

Where? I thought.

"Yes, I do!" Nonna was always the lady.

The other bombshell that my father threw was directed to Carolina and me.

"You're both starting school in couple of days. I've made a booking at the local college."

"How can we go to school? We can't even speak English?"

Once again, my father had decided and was adamant that Carolina and I follow his orders. I was ready to argue, though anything I may have said would have little or no effect on my father. The only thing that gave me courage to keep me going was the thought that somewhere in this vast land there was Michael. So, among discrimination, verbal abuse, insults, and diatribe, life unfolded as it should have.

12

NONNA MARIANNA

Time passed, and we continued to struggle. We hid our pain and humiliation. We did not even want to acknowledge that our self-esteem was nonexistent. We learned to accept what came our way without reaction. Of course, to their own detriment, some people did react, but most of us knew that silence was the only way out. It was as if who we were, our very essence, had been assassinated.

In the first years of residence in the new country we worked and acted like automatons. Our freedom of will had been challenged, and we did as we were told, for doing otherwise would result in name-calling and insults, to say the least.

No! I wasn't going to relate a story that would degrade us right down the ages.

So, I had decided that I wasn't going to continue with the story of the Del Feo family. But my grandchildren had other ideas.

"You must tell us the story, Nonna!"

"It is too painful to remember the struggles of an immigrant," I replied to my granddaughters, who insisted that I should tell them the story of the family. In saying that, my mind went back to when I was a teenager and I had insisted that my grandmother tell me about the lives and vicissitudes of my ancestors.

At first, I was too embarrassed to tell them the undignified circumstances that plagued the life of an immigrant. Having put my personal feelings aside, I realized that they had a right to know. My life's journey was partly their heritage, and since our arrival in Australia, according to my granddaughters, the development of our lives was a history that had to be told. I could also tell my granddaughters that, as most Italians knew, we were not those people that some of the Australian public thought we were. We came from a country that had given the world music, fashion, art, cuisine, and so on. We had gained respect by most of the world and eventually, we had to regain respect by our host country.

Aloud, I said, "As immigrants, we needed to take courage and help build this country regardless of how we felt."

"You all certainly did do just that. I read somewhere that wherever there was work to be done, there were Italians," said my granddaughter, Leah.

"Yes, indeed, they worked even on weekends to build a home for their family. They did the work that no one else wanted to do. The Italians were even disliked by the unions because they wanted to get on with their job—they did not want to strike and waste time. They had come to Australia to work, and work they did."

"But tell us your story, Nonna. Tell us of your achievements. You know that you're our hero?"

My best achievement, and I take pride in it, was when I became a mother. My second-best achievement is not really my own, but I take enormous pride in it anyway. I guess indirectly I am sort of responsible: I am talking about you, my two beautiful granddaughters. You two who are the best result of what a true integration with people should be, an integration born out of love and not out of hatred. Nothing good is born out of hatred; it is love that conquers every obstacle and nurtures the soul. It is thanks to that love that the story continues. And it is definitely the right thing to do—to allow it to continue.

"Of course, it is the right thing to do. Truth has a way of coming out into the light, and when it does, it liberates, Nonna," said Leah.

"Of course, it does. You are so intelligent and wise, both of you. But let's get on with the story, then. A story that overlaps and interacts with the story of others."

As you know, when we arrived in Australia, we had a grandfather who lived here. My mother, your nonnina, as you used to call her, was anxious to see her father. She had not seen him or heard from him since she was twelve years of age. My father (your nonnino) did not want to go with my mother to see my grandfather because they had not parted on friendly terms. My mother decided to catch a taxi to go to his place on the farm. My mother, my sister, and I went. When we arrived there, he was chopping wood. We stood behind him and after a while he must have sensed a presence, for he turned around.

"Who are you? Do I know you?" He asked.

"I'm your daughter, and these are your grandchildren."

He became very pale. My mother went toward him to embrace him, but he pulled back a little and said, "I thought you had decided not to come to Australia anymore, or at least that's what your husband said."

"He had to say that, or else you would have stopped the papers for my mother to come. And if my mother wasn't coming, I would not come either."

"You would have been better off not to come. Australia needs working people and not people like you and your mother who have been used to being served."

"How would you know what we are capable of?" I looked at mother and saw that she was on the verge of tears.

"I think we should go Mamma. The taxi is waiting for us," I said.

Mamma seemed to be in a painful trance. Once again, she had been rejected and hurt. God only knew what this would do to her. All her dreams and hopes had been shattered. Her father had done it again.

"You did not like your grandfather much, did you, Nonna?"

"I didn't either dislike him or like him, but I hated what he did to his family—to his own daughter."

Disillusioned. we went home. On Monday, my sister and I had to face school.

13

CATHOLIC COLLEGE

On Monday morning, Carolina and I walked to school. The Catholic College wasn't very far from where we lived. Of course, I did not understand everything the nun, Mother Theresa, was saying. I understood, though, that she was introducing the two Italian girls to the school. The introduction met with a loud booing from all the pupils. I wanted to run away in that very instant. But, at the same time, something surged within me—a kind of strength. I vowed to myself that I would learn English as well as any of those girls, if not better.

"And you did, Nonna," said Leah.

"It could not have been easy." Jane's voice was sympathetic.

"No, it wasn't. It was hard, especially when every time I spoke a word, I would be ridiculed. Because of my lack of knowledge of the English language, I was placed in a class two years below my level in Italy. That was frustrating because I knew what the teacher wrote on the blackboard, but I was scared to answer, for I was certain of being mocked. So, I spent months without saying a word.

Eventually, when I took courage to put my hand up to answer, at first everyone was staring at me. Then there was a roaring laughter, which put me off ever answering again."

As the months went by, going back to Italy seemed further and further away. My dream of going to university was becoming an impossibility, for as I became older there would be less chance of being accepted into an Italian university. As for Australia, my English would never reach university standard, I thought. But I kept on reading, and I kept on studying. Amid all the turmoil, the dream of finding the love of my life was always in my thoughts.

At school, we were asked to assimilate, to mix and become like other young people, but the other young people wanted nothing to do with us. I soon realized that the idea that immigrants should assimilate was something that the heads of government had requested. The concept of assimilation that the Italian immigrants and those of other nationalities were told to adopt, I observed, could never work.

The meaning of assimilation according to the dictionary is "the process by which immigrants or other newcomers are brought to adopt the attitudes and cultural patterns of the society into which they have come. Cultural patterns and attitudes, a cultural uniformity based on the dominant culture." That would have been the Anglo-Australian culture, of course. We were actually told to become another nationality and create cultural uniformity. Hence, we had to be totally absorbed into another cultural identity.

Of course, to achieve this, we had to become oblivious to our ancient traditions; we had to forget not only who we were and what we knew but also our ancestral heritage. They were, indeed, advocating mindless uniformity.

As time went by, we realized that they were serious about this ludicrous policy. For instance, the men, used as they were to meeting in the Italian piazza, thought they could do the same in Australia. After a day's work, they would gather in a group. It was a harmless ritual that they did to unwind or discuss their favorite sport. However, if they started to talk in their language, they were pushed and told, in no uncertain terms, to split up and go home.

"Couldn't they call the police when they were treated badly?" asked Jane.

"Those people who pushed and shoved were the police. It didn't matter whether one went to an office, a shop, or a bank; the treatment was always the same—very negative and humiliating, to say the least. You could not report anyone because they were almost free to abuse; they had a discriminatory law on their side."

I suppose in the process of assimilation there were a few things we could do. We could start by giving up our cappuccino and replace it with chicory coffee; the plate of pasta had to be exchanged with tinned spaghetti; and the homemade tomato sauce had to be replaced with bottled sweet sauce. Of course, the men could substitute their tailored pants for the very popular bell-bottom pants. But even if the Italians did all those things, they still could be identified in a huge crowd for their dark complexion, or at least that was the common view, I said with a smile, wanting desperately to lighten up the atmosphere for the girls and for myself.

"Not all the Italians are dark, Nonna. You're not!" remarked Leah.

"No! Most of my family, as you know, are tall, blue-eyed blondes. The reason why Australia, with its "all-white policy" first tried to reject southern European migrants was because they were dark. But then, since they needed to populate Australia, and they needed skilled workers, they allowed them into the country."

The Italians, in order to please, did give up a few things that were part of their character. For instance, they did try to stop talking with their hands, to the point where it was difficult for them to speak any language at all; they tried to stop singing while working; and stopped being generally happy.

"Nonna, you are joking, aren't you?" asked Leah with a hint of anger in her voice.

"I'm not, really. I just have never understood why they wanted us to assimilate, especially since they did not like us very much."

"Did that upset you? I mean the fact that they didn't like you—Italians, I mean," asked Jane. She sounded emotional.

"At first, yes, but then my pride helped me to get over it. I wasn't going to lie down and die just because some people were discriminatory and xenophobic."

"So, what did you do?"

"I decided to be myself, the best I could be." I had the background and the upbringing to be able to do almost whatever I chose.

"From what you're saying then, Nonna, assimilation didn't work," stated Leah.

"No! It didn't. It's wrong to become like other people, anyway. The person lives a lie all his or her life."

"What happened then?" asked Jane.

When assimilation didn't work, it was thought that integration might. The notion of integration, in my opinion, was no better than that of assimilation. Normally, the concept of integration was used to abolish racial segregation, but it does not seem to have done that. The policy of integration allowed any immigrants into Australia, but they had to adopt the Anglo culture in public. However, they were permitted to resume their own culture at home. So, in a sense, the immigrants were asked to integrate and become instantly invisible by day and visible by night, except that this had to be done behind closed doors. But, as far as we were concerned, being invisible was not part of the Italian character.

Paradoxical as it may seem, while the government insisted that we should integrate, at the same time the people did not accept us, and we felt shunned. When people are disliked and pushed away, it is obvious that they withdraw within themselves, and the opposite happens: after a while they become marginalized. This happened to many Italians, especially to women who stayed at home to look after their children. They were made to feel dejected and hence became depressed. Because they could not speak the language, they felt useless and inadequate. I was the interpreter for many of those ladies, and the doctors never failed to prescribe Librium nearly every time I brought someone for an examination, whether she had a headache or sore foot. My mother was no exception; she became addicted to the dreaded tranquilizers.

The men, however, because they had to go out to work had a better chance of a kind of subsistence; they could learn some English. If they weren't accepted, they were at least tolerated. No one cared about people's well-being. No one realized that if immigrants were welcomed by the host country and allowed to do the work they were asked to, they would eventually and naturally integrate, but it could not happen overnight; it would take a few generations of mixed marriages.

"Did you make friends at school, Nonna?"

"Just a few, only those that were in the same predicament. Some of the sons and daughters of the Italians who had migrated before us appeared to prefer not to be recognized of being of Italian origin. They did not want to speak Italian for fear of being reprimanded and mocked. I guess if they did speak Italian, they would be called dingoes, wogs, or dagos. These were the names by which we were addressed."

"Nonna, that's awful," my granddaughters said. "You must hate Australia!"

"Yes, it was awful! And no, I don't hate Australia; on the contrary, I actually love Australia. We Italians have touched and nurtured the soil. We have built on it. We have contributed toward the development of the nation, and to a certain extent, even if some of the first-generation immigrants couldn't, our children have become part of the country. It only needed time and patience to allow people to do naturally what force and degradation could never achieve. One should never trample on peoples' dignity. As I said before, I felt sure that integration would have happened, but it needed time, love, and patience for it to come about."

"You are right, Nonna!" said Leah vehemently.

"Things have changed now. We are a multicultural society," said Jane.

"Yes, they have changed! Multiculturalism is now in place, and it has challenged the concept of assimilation. I do hope things have changed, I really and sincerely hope so. Sometimes though, policy and public attitude are poles apart."

Unfortunately, discrimination, even though it is against the law, still exists. For instance, as I said, we are tolerated. The word "tolerate" is used even now by Australian people when talking about other cultures. "One must tolerate," is often said. "Tolerance" appears to have a concept of superiority in its meaning. The person who tolerates feels superior to the one who is tolerated. Tolerate: "to allow someone to do something you don't approve of; to accept something unpleasant without becoming impatient or angry; to accept someone without welcoming them or liking them; to put up with something or someone you don't particularly care for, so you bear and suffer that particular person or thing. For instance, to tolerate another person's religion or another person's nationality implies disapproval."

It appears, then, that there is no equality in tolerance. In fact, we can go, as far as to say that there is no true acceptance in tolerance.

Acceptance: "favorable reception; approval; the fact of allowing someone to become part of a group or community and making them feel welcome."

"To become part of the whole, one has to be accepted for what one is," admitted Leah.

"I thought Italians were accepted now," reflected Jane.

"I think so, too. After all, most of our children and grandchildren, like you, are either students or university graduates, and they would not tolerate discrimination of any sort, but other immigrants are not totally immune. The antidiscrimination law, however, will enable immigrants to demand to be treated like human beings. Soon or later, we have to realize that people belong to the same globe and have a right to be anywhere, given of course that they observe the law of the land."

"I think we can learn so much from other cultures," said Leah, wisely.

"Of course, we can! For instance, Sicily has had different people and numerous civilizations, such as the Greeks, the Byzantine, the Arabs, the Normans, the Angevin and Swabian, the Aragonese, and Spanish and so on. Not counting the immigrants and refugees that it has had and given asylum to over the years. Each civilization is still visible in the churches, temples, and mosque. History says that the Great Emperor Frederic II of Sicily (1194–1250) gave permission for a mosque to be built in Palermo, and that at his court four different languages were spoken. Very open and accepting of strangers, don't you think?"

"So, before Australia you lived in a multicultural society, Nonna?" asked Jane.

"You may say that, except that we didn't use the words 'multicultural society.' That's a concept from other countries that was adopted by Australia. Actually, after hundreds of years of the different cultures being together in Sicily, we became one society, not forgetting though our heritage visible in the different buildings and the variety of delicious foods. In a few hundred years it will be the same in Australia. It will happen gradually when immigrants are made to feel at home, and their children's children, without a doubt, will call Australia home."

"Even though you are a first-generation Italian, do you call Australia home?" asked Jane.

"Yes!"

"Why?"

"We shall discuss this subject another time."

"Why not now?"

"Because this argument brings back the painful memories of a very cruel history. Its cruel repercussions, even though many intentionally forget it, continue to affect peoples' lives. Racism, because it disrespects the human person, has to be always wrong and unforgivable."

"Can we please leave this discussion for now? Instead, I shall tell you about my family."

"We know all about your family, our ancestors in Sicily. We learned that from your first book, The Island of the Elyms, but we don't know much about the family in Australia. You have told us about your grandfather on your arrival in Australia, but you haven't told us much about your grandmother or about your mother and your father."

"Yes, please, Nonna, tell us about your family and our family." The girls were emphatic about wanting to hear about the Del Feo family.

14

THE SHORT LIFE OF A BEAUTIFUL LADY

Donna Camilla, your great-great-grandmother, was a magnificent lady. Everyone respected her. Of course, the respect was mutual; she had a good word for everyone. Her stay in Australia was a sad one. I always thought that she should have stayed back in Sicily where everyone knew her, and she was highly esteemed.

My mother's quest to gather the family together and to live happily ever after did not work. My grandmother suffered in silence. Did she hope for a reunion with her husband? We will never know. One thing was certain; she must have suffered an enormous humiliation to know that her husband was so near and yet so far. I am sure that she did not worry for herself so much, but the fact that he had the ruthlessness to repudiate his own daughter and his granddaughters would have slowly killed her.

We moved to the city of Perth about ten years after arriving in Australia. It was I who wanted to move to the city before my two beautiful girls, Natalie Eleonora and Marie Teresa, went to school. Carolina had married the love of her life and when we left the country town, she already had a baby boy; a girl was to follow a few years later. In Perth, my children, I thought, would have better options than in a country town; they would have the opportunity to go to university. Since I couldn't, I guess I wanted to live my dream through my own children.

In Perth we were, if not happy, fairly content. Everyone had a job. My mother who was a multiskilled person, worked first as a dressmaker and then as a cook in a hotel. My nonna acted as a housekeeper for all of us: Dalle stelle alla stalla (from the stars to the stable), says an Italian proverb. All her life she had been served and now she herself was the servant. She did it willingly, though, and with great love. And we in turn adored her. She was such an excellent cook. Actually, all the Del Feo women were excellent cooks.

I was glad we had put some distance between our family and my grandfather—out of sight out of mind, as the saying goes. My mother became more depressed and more attached to the Librium tablets. Then, because of health reasons, she gave up her job. My nonna continued to cook, and I helped her anytime I could. First, with Carmela back in Sicily and now with Nonna, I also became a proficient cook to the point where it became one of my passions. The other passion of course was studying, and I did that in any spare time I had.

"I love cooking also," said Jane.

"I know you both do. It runs in the family."

"But please, Nonna, continue with your nonna's story. Did she like Australia?"

"I don't know! She never went out. Except for the occasional visitor, she had no contact with people."

One day a telegram arrived. It was from my grandfather, who wanted to come to Perth to spend his last years with his family. Apparently, the woman who lived with him had left him. He was sick and had no one to care for him. My mother awoke from the torpor she was in because of her depression and tranquilizers and decided she would go to her father's farm and bring him back with her to Perth.

"Why are you doing that?" I asked.

"Because he is my father." I thought I would never hear that meaningless dictum again that I had heard all my life. But here it was, my mother was going to reunite the family again. What a laugh!

"Did you discuss this with Papà?" I asked her.

"Yes, and he said to do whatever my conscience dictates."

"What about Nonna?"

"Who?"

"Nonna! Your mother! Remember her?" I said sarcastically.

"Of course, I do! I also told her that I was going to bring my father home where he belongs."

"He doesn't belong here! And what did she say?"

"Who?"

"Your mother, that's who."

"She didn't say anything much. She said it was my house, and I could bring whoever I like into it."

"And you thought that was a happy consent on her part?"

"She should be happy. I'm bringing her husband back home to her."

"No! You are not. You are bringing a stranger back home to her."

"That's enough! It has been decided. I am leaving early tomorrow morning to pick him up."

"Who with? You can't drive."

"I have already made arrangements. Your father's cousin has volunteered to drive me."

"So, you are going to do this?"

"Of course, I am. It's settled," she repeated.

My mother's assertiveness was very unusual. I hoped it would last for other circumstances.

A few days later they arrived. My grandfather had all his luggage with him, which wasn't much considering all the years he had been in Australia. At lunch he talked about his past; I think he realized that he was a stranger in this household. He must have wondered, as we did, what on earth he was doing here. He kept on talking, maybe to cover up his embarrassment. I noticed also that he was uncomfortable with Italian culture and that he had been almost absorbed into the Australian way of life. However, he spoke in defense of the Italians, perhaps to impress us.

We heard about the time when he was sent to an internment camp. All the Italians were; we heard about how many houses belonging to Italians were set on fire because they were considered enemies of war.

"They did this to innocent people because all the Italians in Australia had nothing to do with the war," he said. For this I had to agree, knowing how thoroughly we had been screened before we were admitted as migrants. If migrants had so much as a fine in their records, they would not be allowed in the country. Once again, we had been victimized by the host country, which, because it had allowed us to come, should have had the diplomacy to welcome us instead of our being made into second-class citizens.

Life was cruel on a personal level and on a social level. Because my grandmother was a true lady, she said hello to my grandfather on the rare occasion that they met. I knew she was uncomfortable in his company, though.

"Are you OK, Nonna?" I asked.

"Yes," she replied, but I knew she was only saying that in order not to make me feel sad.

One of the most dignified ladies I have ever known looks as if her dignity has been taken away, I thought.

My grandfather, since he was sick, stayed in his room and was served his meals there. When on occasion he came out, my Nonna stayed in her room. Lately I had noticed that my Nonna wasn't looking too well. We called the doctor and as he examined her, he shook his head and said she had to be hospitalized. A few days later I was called by the specialist—he wanted to talk to me. He told me that there was nothing they could do and that my darling Nonna had only a couple of months to live. It would be better if she spent the last days at home. I was devastated; my dearest nonna was going to die. She wasn't old; I thought she still had years ahead of her.

Ironically, while my grandmother came home, my grandfather was hospitalized. They were never to see each other again. As the doctors had predicted, before the two months were up, Nonna breathed her last breath in my arms. When a family friend went to the hospital to tell my grandfather the news, we were told he cried. As destiny would have it, he wasn't able to be at my grandmother's funeral. A few weeks later he came back home, where he lived a couple of years before he also passed away.

15

SHE SANG AND DANCED NO MORE

"Girls, you're crying."

"No, we're not," they answered in unison.

"The story of my nonna made you sad, didn't it?"

"It is a sad story, especially when someone has lived a totally unhappy life." Leah's blue eyes sparkled with tears.

"There were times back in Sicily when my nonna was content."

"Nonna, please continue with the story of your mamma's life," pleaded Jane.

"I don't think I should. I don't want you to be upset, because my mamma's life story is a sad one also."

"I remember Nonnina. She was a very beautiful lady, wasn't she?" Leah was remembering.

"I don't remember her very well. I remember that everyone said she was beautiful and tall and that it was unusual for a Sicilian. To be tall, I mean, at least that's what I heard," said Jane.

"Yes, many people said she was not a typical Sicilian. What is the common characteristic of Sicilians? The Australian definition was unequivocally clear and precise: short, dark, and fat. If this definition is correct, then those people were right. She was, most assuredly, none of those things. On the contrary, as we said, she was tall, slim, with light brown hair and hazel eyes, which at times appeared green. She always dressed elegantly and in the latest fashion, and I often thought that she was the most beautiful lady I had ever seen. Some people thought she looked like a baroness; little did they know that she really was a baroness. This was the only well-kept secret of our family.

"One should not generalize about people being a certain type. Contrary to what was said about Sicilians, all the members of our family are tall. Anyway, the young people in Sicily seem also to be fairly tall. Probably, after the war there was less poverty and better nutrition. Who knows? We are digressing, though."

"Yes, we are, let's get back to Nonnina."

As you said before, you already know Nonnina's early life in Sicily. When I was young, she appeared really happy. She sang and danced with us, but then the vicissitudes of life changed her from courageous to fearful, from happy to sad. Before we left Sicily, she worked frantically; she quickly sold properties, packed huge trunks, putting in them what she could and giving away the rest. I remember distinctly the many family heirlooms and precious antiques disposed of without a second thought and without distress or tears.

In a flash hundreds of years of history had been obliterated, indeed an end of an era. Come to think of it, she did not flinch or cry when she left Sicily, the beautiful island with myriads of colors, the enchanted Island of Cyclops and nymphs, as the Homeric legend would have it. Even though she was sure this bewitching island in the middle of the Mediterranean would never be her home again, she was inflexible in her decision to leave it. The reason: to bring the family together, no doubt.

The land to which she had arrived was barren—without shade from the scorching sun, and without tall mountains or deep valleys; everything was flat and red or a sunburned brown.

"The weather is hot," she said, "but there is no warmth on people's faces, at least not for us."

She detested the fact that migrants were considered people of poor socioeconomic condition who had little or no education. While this was probably true for some, it was most definitely not true of her. However, she was aware that because she lacked fluency in the English language, she would be considered illiterate, uneducated, and backward. This knowledge anguished her immensely. From that day on, she rarely smiled. And whatever semblance of a smile remained, that also was to wither and die.

Over the years she had learned some English but spoke very little of it for fear of being ridiculed. As time went by, the pride that had made her hold her head high was gone. She became introspective, self-conscious, and lonely, and her loneliness, paradoxically, could not be overcome by the company of family and friends. Gradually, as if she had remained encapsulated in time and place, she became inhibited and alienated and lost touch with both cultures. She lost her song and the joie de vivre.

16

UNHAPPY AND CONFUSED

Through struggles and hardships, one by one, the years went by. On my mother's beautiful face were now the deep signs of a pessimistic melancholy. Her days were dismal and gloomy and filled with despair; her outlook on life became progressively more negative. Very soon she became depressed, a depression so severe that it changed her personality completely. She became totally dependent on her now married children. She sought attention by feigning every ailment and disease imaginable. She went to doctors and specialists in the hope that they would find something physically wrong with her, and when they never did, she grew impatient with them.

Eventually, she only went to those doctors who prescribed sedatives and tranquilizers. As I said before, she became addicted to drugs, but instead of becoming calmer she became increasingly more unhappy and agitated. She felt continually threatened and developed fears of every description: fear of disease, fear of accidents, fears of tragedies and disasters, fear of death, and so on. She was anxious about every task she performed, from cooking dinner, shopping for it, or doing the washing. Routine chores that she had done repeatedly became enormous undertakings for which she sought continuous help from her daughters, Carolina and me. At parties, the lady who once had loved to entertain could not interact with others and sat quietly in a corner. If she had any joy at all, it came from her four grandchildren, whom she dearly loved: my two girls and Carolina's boy and a girl, and later, of course from her great-grandchildren, whom she adored.

"I remember that so clearly," said Leah. "But please continue, Nonna Marianna."

"Yes, please continue," echoed Jane.

"One day, though, aware that she was losing her memory, she became extremely distressed and frightened. However, when she had difficulties in carrying out a conversation and had problems with spatial-temporal orientation, it was the family who became worried and concerned. The diagnosis was, without a doubt, the much dreaded Alzheimer's disease. Unfortunately, this time it was not an imaginary disease caused by her hypochondria, as in the past, but it was a real and cruel disease, and it was frightening. This atrocious illness was a downward journey of gradual deterioration whereby each of the human faculties failed, but what was worse, it appeared to take away every shred of dignity and intellect—at least, so I thought at that time.

"Very soon sheer terror replaced the perennial sadness in her eyes. The terror was caused by horrible auditory and visual hallucinations. Around her she saw animals of every kind, from huge serpents to tigers and lions."

"Marianna, there's a huge tiger in the backyard. And what's that lion doing there?" We were told by the doctors not to contradict her because that might cause frustrations, so we went along and pretended that we saw what she did. Inanimate and familiar objects took the semblance of snakes.

"Marianna, what is that snake doing around your neck?" This time my reflexes got the better of me and I jumped and pulled away the scarf I was wearing around my neck.

Other times she saw crowds of limbless people with vicious, distorted, and ugly faces and menacing sardonic grins.

"Who cut the arm off that woman and bruised her? She is bleeding all over. And look at the man—someone chopped his leg off."

Her life had become a constant horror movie, except that for her it was a reality. Her face reflected the continual turmoil produced by those violent hallucinations that kept her in the grip of fear in a Hades-like labyrinth without apparent escape.

"Oh, how awful, Nonna!" The girls looked apprehensive.

"Yes, it was." It was pitiful for us, the members of the family, to be witnesses to each stage and progression of the disease that manifested in the gradual regression of our loved one.

The next phase would be the alteration of her personality and temperament, whereby, in all probability, she would become aggressive toward members of the family and people in general. Such had been the warning of doctors and the description of the disease in textbooks. But I failed to see how such a gentle and loving lady could have such a dramatic change of personality, and I also could not believe that she could become violent and aggressive toward anyone, let alone members of her family. Whether this was the general manifestation of the disease or not, I was sure it would not happen to her.

In fact, it did not. On the contrary, one day, as if coming back into the light after being in a dark abyss, a glimmer of a smile appeared on her face, and her features seemed more relaxed. Her hallucinations had gradually become more benevolent and friendlier. Now smiling people and children whom she constantly wanted to feed and take care of populated her backyard.

"Marianna, that little girl must be hungry by now, give her something to eat. Marianna, quickly, the little girl is starving; give her something to eat. She could also do with some new clothes, go out and buy her some new dresses." To appease my mother, my days were full of pretense.

One day she appeared comforted by the presence of heavenly bodies; one in particular she recognized as her mother, who had been dead for many years. It was as if her mother were encouraging her and helping her to make the transition from the earthly existence into the eternal ecstasy.

"Look over there, Marianna! Can you see our lady Mary?" I wished I could.

One by one, as if the disease was gradually and gently transporting her back in time, her fears left her.

Eventually, when she had to be placed in a nursing home, she was eager to go because she thought she was returning home. And indeed, she acted as if the huge house with many rooms was her home back in Sicily. She dressed elegantly; she smiled politely, spoke with extreme courtesy, and wanted to entertain her visitors. She progressively lost all cultural barriers and inhibitions and became happier and at peace with herself.

One day when she was asked how old she was, she replied convincingly: "Sixteen." All the men in the nursing home, as back in Sicily, became her suitors courting her. Paradoxical as it may seem, her Alzheimer's disease had erased every trace of the brutal existence of the present, and it had taken her back to the time when she was happy and carefree. In a sense, it had given back her pride and self-esteem. Once again, she was the gracious lady of the manor, so to speak.

She had traveled the full circle. She had fought, she had struggled, she had loved, she had prayed, and she had returned home. It was then that I knew for certain that she would not be with us much longer. One evening at dusk, without jolts and without pain and with great dignity, she slipped away to her eternal home. As I looked at her delicate and ethereal features, amid sobs and tears, I remember whispering: "You are the most beautiful lady I have ever seen, Mamma."

17

Papà Is Left Alone

My father was different from my mother. He was sure of himself; perhaps during the war, being a prisoner in a German camp and living among different cultures had made him strong to deal with the animosity that we had found in Australia. He did not care much whether he was liked or not. He went about doing his work of a master craftsman, looked after his family, paid his taxes, obeyed the law, and paid no attention to anything that might perturb his life. He was a man of the world and understood that people wanting to think themselves superior put down others. This, he thought, was due to a lack of understanding of humanity at large and as a result fearing different civilizations. He always told me, "Marianna, if you do the right thing by people, eventually they will respect you."

"It was true what Nonnino said, Nonna, everyone who knows you respects you," said Leah.

"I remember Nonnino." Jane was happy that finally she could be part of the story.

"Of course, you do. He loved both of you very much. There was nothing he would not do for his grandchildren and his great-grandchildren."

When my sister and I were young back in Sicily, my father was rather authoritative with us. He did not show much affection—never a hug or a kiss. When we attempted to kiss him, he would turn his cheek to be kissed. Maybe a custom of the time. It seems that showing affection would appear a kind of weakness on the father's part. He, the head of the household, as he was made to believe, had to appear intransigent.

However, when we arrived in Australia, he gradually lost his rigorous ways and steadily became almost lenient. I think it was a kind of guilt for having taken us away from a place where we had everything, and here we had nothing. We had to start from scratch to create part of what we had left behind. Papà worked at two jobs and eventually owned a beautiful home.

We all worked and contributed toward the building of the home. Carolina and I worked part time because Papà was adamant that we should go to school. He said we had to recapture for ourselves and for our family what emigration had taken away from us, so an education, and particularly the knowledge of the English language, was essential. Of course, since I loved studying, I did not have to be told twice.

As far as my father was concerned, though, I was a little too exaggerated with the books and he wanted me to balance my life by learning housework in order that one day I would make a good wife. I told him that I did not have to learn housework since women knew how to do it—it was innate with them, we were taught to believe. At least in those times, the time when we arrived in Australia, men's and women's roles were specific—the man went to work and provided for the family while the woman ran the household, children, and husband included, without the husband being aware, of course.

As I was saying, my father, because he did not fear anyone, got on with everyone. He invited people home for meals and with the exquisite cooking in our household, they had to like us, if not for ourselves, then for our cuisine; one could see that the people wanted to be invited again and again.

Being a blue-eyed blond, my father was thought to be a northern European. I never told him, but I had this sneaky suspicion that his looks were partly the reason why he was liked. Actually, I must be candid and say that even if we told people we came from Sicily, at that time not many knew whether Sicily was a country, an island, or a person. So, early in our Australian challenge, we escaped mafia jokes. Needless to say, they came later.

Back to my father. He had friends of every nationality and helped everyone in need and the ones not so needy. He was jovial and cordial with everyone, women in particular, but not so that he would desecrate his marriage vows. When it came to love, he only had eyes for Eleonora, his beautiful wife, and she in turn only had eyes for him. Australia had been good for their marriage. Being away from my father's meddling sisters, their relationship had gained a salutary momentum. They were so much an item that when my mother passed away, my father appeared lost. That seemed strange for such a strong man—a man who had survived the atrocities of the Second World War.

Papà used to tell us some of the stories of the war. I remember him showing us a key that he had brought back from the German prison camp. It seems that he was given the key to a warehouse where potatoes were kept to fix some windows, which the loud bang of the bombs had shattered. Among the debris he had found a rusty key, which enabled him to make a copy of the warehouse key. At night he would crawl in, and with his comrades would steal a potato each. They would not dare steal more than one for fear of being found out, which would have meant instant death. The potato was a feast for them because the prisoners were accustomed to searching in the bins for scraps and mostly found potato skins to curb their hunger a little.

One day there was a rumor that the war was ending. In the camp things were out of control. My father took the chance and escaped and walked from Germany to Italy. He desperately wanted to get away from potential war zones, and vowed never to go to war again.

"As long as I live," he had said, "I do not want to witness such destructive hostilities that people are forced to have toward each other." Hence, the emigration to Australia—Australia was thought to be a safe country. And so it was. So, my father has had a happy life in Australia.

When my Mamma passed away, as I was saying, Papà became subdued and unresponsive, very much like he was after the war in Sicily. But after a period, his old self resurfaced, his exuberant personality could not be held back. He traveled to Sicily every couple of years and enjoyed a peaceful existence. Family and friends, both in Australia and in Sicily, surrounded him.

We all got together for meals that he prepared. We also gathered for important occasions such as birthdays, Christmas, and Easter. On those days, even though we worked hard, we also had fun and were filled with happiness. The preparations seemed as important as the actual eating. Papà took charge where my mother had done so before. Different nationalities of people started to join us on those days when the wonderful smells of the different foods filled the air in the entire neighborhood, or so we were told. People started to enjoy the spaghetti with fresh tomato sauce. Where previously garlic produced a "stench" in the Italian people, now everyone started to enjoy the flavor of garlic. The old joke that Italians didn't have freckles because the olive oil they consumed made the freckles slide off their skin, now nearly everybody was enjoying olive oil, and very soon there would be no freckles on anyone's skin.

History has given us Sicilians an unpleasant reputation when it comes to food and eating. It seems that Plato on his voyages to Sicily judged that the Sicilians were "committed to fill their stomach with food twice a day and at night they never slept alone." Similarly, the Greek philosopher Empedocles (circa 493–433 BC), who lived in Sicily, said, "The citizens were real barbarians seeing that they ate as if they were going to die the following day." Because of the opinion of these illustrious gentlemen, we have been left with the reputation of over-indulging and therefore afflicted with one of the seven deadly sins, the cardinal sin of gluttony.

I beg to differ, though, with these highly regarded philosophers of all ages. Sicilians love the ecstasy and the elation of preparation of the food and not necessarily the eating. For a particular occasion, they prepare enough to feed the five thousand. They have many baskets left for weeks to come and hence, four or five fridges and freezers in their home. My family is a living proof that they don't eat everything they prepare because almost every member is quite slim, me included. Not counting the matriarchs that we had had in our family, of course; they had to be big to exert their authority.

As usual, I have digressed; so let's return to the story.

Thanks to my father and to many Italians like him, who were kind and hospitable to everyone, we were starting to come together in friendship in this huge land called Australia.

"Of course, we have a long way to go to conquer the hearts of the people of Australia," said Papà, "but eventually it will happen, there is no doubt about it. Indeed, it will happen!"

We thought my father would last forever. Anyone who had survived the carnage of war appeared indestructible. But since no one is, my father eventually became ill and was given a pretty bleak diagnosis. His prognosis was he did not have long to live. I felt that our time together—the time when we became close—was brief.

It was not only he who was at fault. But was he really at fault or was he doing the best he knew how as a father? Certainly, he had been strict, but he thought he was doing the right thing. I, on the other hand, should have understood instead of feeling unloved. He did love me as I loved him, but I needed to tell him that before it was too late, before I would be left feeling remorse for the rest of my life.

One day I threw my arms around him and told him I loved him. What a wonderful moment that was. He told me he was ready to go. He had had a good life, and now the time had come to join Mamma. I sobbed and said, "Please forgive me, Papà."

"There's nothing to forgive; you have been a good daughter." One evening when the family was gathered, it was he who said he had to talk to us.

"I know that I have not been a very expressive father," he said, "but it wasn't that I didn't love you all. On the contrary, I love you very much. I just had not been brought up to show affection. For those times," he continued, "you might have thought that I was an uncaring father. From the bottom of my heart, I'm sincerely sorry." As he spoke, he had tears in his eyes. That was something totally new to me and to all of us. We also sobbed. It was such an amazing moment. We were reassured that we always knew he loved us, and he had been a good father.

Carolina and I asked if there was something we could do for him. We meant if there was something to make the last moments of his life a little more comfortable, but we did not have the courage to say so. However, he understood:

"If it's possible," he said, "I don't want to die in a hospital bed. I would prefer to stay at home."

Carolina and I looked at one another and said at the same time, "It shall be done. We shall bring doctors and nurses home to make sure you're not in any pain."

And so it was. He passed away holding my sister's hand on one side and mine on the other, leaving behind a legacy of love. Everyone who knew him admired him—he had left behind a history of Italian tradition at its best—a tradition that eventually would be amalgamated into the Australian culture—or should I say integrated?

18

A Multicultural Society

With multiculturalism, a policy was established that allowed any immigrants into Australia, no matter the nationality, race, or creed. Everyone could keep their own customs if they observed the Australian law. Although the policy was put in place in 1972, its application and acceptance has been a gradual process.

We had already started to make many friends. They came to visit and seemed to enjoy our hospitality. We realized we could learn so much from one another. At parties we were all mixed—we were starting to appreciate our multicultural society. It was not because a government had said that we should assimilate or integrate, but because we were getting to know one another and were becoming aware of one another's differences and fundamentally recognizing each other's similarities, which were many.

We were God's children on the same planet and citizens of the same world. Yes, we had become Australians, but finally we were allowed to share cultures instead of being told to forget who we were. If that had not happened, how much poorer we would all have been? Australia could not boast, as it can now, for instance, that on its soil people of different cultures are learning to live in harmony.

It has not been easy, and at times we still encounter discriminations, but we learned not to be hurt by them.

"Did the insults have lasting effect on you? Did they leave scars for a lifetime?" asked Leah.

"Were you scarred for life, Nonna?" repeated Jane. There was a tone of compassion in her voice.

"Many people were affected. I, on the other hand, tried desperately not to allow it to totally annihilate my personality. So, I don't think I was scarred for life. There were two things I could have done—become perennially depressed like many others or fight the narrow-mindedness and overcome it."

Of course, it does still upset me, though, when I encounter discrimination and racism whether it is directed toward us or another nationality. I know what it is like to be trampled and humiliated and I do not want anyone else to suffer it. No one has the right to make anyone feel demeaned. I hold no grudges for what I went through—holding grudges is self-destructive. I very soon realized that if I allowed myself to have a feeling of resentment, my psychological well-being would suffer. Of course, I was temporarily hurt and upset, but then I would try to put the incident that had hurt me out of my mind. It was just another opinion, after all.

Deep down, I think I knew that one day we would accept one another. In a sense, I foresaw that a natural integration would start eventually, and to a certain extent, it started before the birth of multiculturalism. Our Sicilian background had shown us that this was inevitable. In fact, on such a small Island for hundreds of years have lived almost all the different cultures of the world. "Discover Sicily and discover the world," it is said. Long ago, we had realized that we could enrich ourselves without totally changing ourselves. But for those people who enjoyed the degradation of other human beings, finally we had a law to protect us against their discriminatory vilification.

Australia's first anti-discrimination law, the 1975 (Cth), aims to ensure that Australians of all backgrounds are treated equally and have the same opportunities. The law protects people across Australia from discrimination on the ground of race, colour, descent, national or ethnic origin, and immigration status. The act also makes racial vilification against the law. This gives additional protection to people who are being publicly and openly offended, insulted, humiliated or intimidated because of their race, colour, or national or ethnic origin. The act gives effect to Australian's obligations under the International Convention on the Elimination of All Forms of Racial Discrimination, to which Australia is committed.

(www.humanrights.gov.au/about/legislation)

"So, no more giving up the traditions of each culture?" asked Leah.

"No. Our traditions that had served us well for generations had to be kept and passed on to our children. I mean those things that have made us who we really are. I feel the same way about other cultures; we can learn so much from them, and Australia offers enormous potential. If only we would abolish our superior attitude. No one is better than others, just different.

"I think we deserve respect because we have earned it. We endured, we worked, we were kind to people, we obeyed the law and patiently waited until the day when we were not just immigrants, but accepted as fellow citizens, neighbors, and ultimately friends. It was the host country that had to accept us; we had no animosity toward Australia and Australians. We came to this country ready to do a job as we had been asked to do, and that we did. Italians did the work that no one else wanted. We could have lost our self-esteem, and many people temporarily did. But then when we had built our beautiful homes and our children had graduated from university, our pride was restored. We finally had a spot in this great land. We had earned it, and no one could take it away from us!"

"It has happened! Everyone respects Italians now!" exclaimed Jane.

"It is discriminatory not to." Leah appeared a little put out.

"Yes, at last we have a law to protect us. Finally, prejudice, discrimination and racism have been outlawed."

"Indeed, we have come a long way, if not in practice, at least in theory. The policies put in place have made giant leaps toward a more humane civilization of the country.

"As we have seen, first there was a white Australia policy, which permitted only white people into the country. Then we had the assimilation policy, which allowed any immigrants into Australia if they adopted an Anglo culture and left behind their old culture.

"This was followed by the integration policy, which permitted any immigrants into Australia if they adopted an Anglo culture and kept it in public while they were allowed to celebrate their own cultures at home.

"Finally, we have the multicultural policy, which allowed any immigrants into Australia permitting them to keep their own culture as long as they followed the Australian law."

Except from criminals, we all knew that we had to obey the law of the land. I think we did that from the start, since the Australian law wasn't that different from the law of other countries, anyway. I think most of us knew the difference from right and wrong.

19

The Life of Nonna Marianna

"And now, Nonna, let's talk about you. Has life in Australia been worthwhile? Have you any regrets?"

"My life in Australia has been different from the one I would have had in Sicily, I am quite certain of that. The fact that I was taken away from everything I knew, from everything I would have been, made me angry toward my father, at first. I thought that his action to take us away from our home, our friends, and our land, had been selfish and misguided."

As the time went by, I realized that his choice was not self-serving but that of a father who wanted the best for his family. He wanted that peace that, because of his fear of the rekindling of the war and other negative family issues, he could not have in Sicily. I also realized that I was too young to make the choice as to where I would spend my life. This could happen later, making choices I mean. I knew, however, that the longer I stayed in Australia, the less, likely it was for me to return and live in the land where I was born.

So, on our arrival, I went to school, and I worked part time in a shop. It did not take too long for me to learn English. I think after three months I was able to have a conversation. Regardless of whether I could pronounce the words properly or not, whether I was ridiculed or not, I persisted in talking English. I told myself that the people who ridiculed me did not know nearly three languages as I did. Hence, if they went to Europe, they would have been worse off than I was.

"So, you didn't mind being bullied?" I could feel that Leah's anger was getting worse.

Perhaps I should stop telling the negative things of my life story, I thought. Yet, I felt that those negatives had made me stronger and aware those words can be like swords and that they can really hurt. Leah was not unlike me, and she would use the knowledge to help others. So, I continued.

"It's not that I didn't mind, but I realized that reaction would have been wrong. As the saying goes, 'The chain reaction of evil— hate begetting hate, wars producing wars—must be broken, or else we shall be plunged into the dark abyss of annihilation.'"

I had seen hate and wars and I had seen the dark abyss that people had been plunged in. I was not going to subject myself to such feelings where someone would be annihilated, even if it were a psychological annihilation. So, I decided that I personally, as much as I could, would break the chain reaction. I would see people in the beauty of the different colors, in the richness of the different cultures, and in the wisdom of the different beliefs. And in doing so I would see their hearts, and that would tell me who they really were. I hoped, one day, they would see me for what I really was, but that didn't have much importance. My job was not for people to like me, but for me to like them.

"You are amazing, Nonna," said Leah.

"Yes, you are!" repeated Jane, who liked everyone to get on with one another.

"I have always been of the belief that if I wanted things to change, I should change myself. And if I changed myself by respecting people and seeing the positive in them, then that might also set off a chain reaction.

"But let us continue with the subject of what has happened in my life rather than what I would have liked to happen. As I was saying, school and work were the major events of my life. I was always determined to learn, not just to be able to speak English in a way that I could be understood, but in a learned way, with the ability of being capable to think in the language, speak the language, and write intelligently.

So, I learned verbs, made up sentences and spoke them out loud. I soon read books, did translations, and felt comfortable speaking it. The dream of my going to university, though, was becoming more impossible by the day. Dreams are what they are, just dreams. Reality is somewhat different."

"What did you do then?" asked Jane.

"Then I got married, and as you know I had two beautiful children: your mother and your auntie."

"You were young when you got married, weren't you, Nonna?" asked Leah.

"Yes, I was very young, but that didn't stop me from dedicating myself to my beautiful family. I knew that my girls had the potential to do whatever they chose. I was adamant that when they were older they could look back without regrets. I guess I wanted them to have the opportunity I didn't have. Before they went to school, we moved from the country town where we lived to the city. The city would offer better opportunities. So, once again, we sold our possessions and the whole family left for the great unknown.

"The move was good for everyone and soon we were living a reasonably decent life. I had a husband who adored me, and the children were doing well at school."

"I know Nonno loves you very much. I actually have never seen two people so much in love," said Leah.

"Nonno does not come from Sicily, does he?" asked Jane.

"No, he comes from the Lazio region, a town near Rome, doesn't he, Nonna?" said Leah.

"Yes! You are correct."

"Did you meet him in Italy or in Australia?" Jane loved a romantic story.

"Neither."

"What do you mean neither? You told me that before you came to Australia, you had never been anywhere else except Sicily."

"That's true, Leah."

"What do you mean, that's true? If you did not meet Nonno in Italy, and you did not meet him in Australia, where did you meet him? In the middle of the ocean?" joked Leah laughingly.

"Yes!

"Did you come on the same ship?"

"No."

"What do you mean, no?"

"No, I did not come on the same ship, and yes, Nonno and I met on the ship."

"Are you purposely trying to confuse me?" said Leah with a smile.

"I thought you had met Nonno in Australia." Jane looked perplexed.

"No, as I said before, we met on the ship named Australia, not in Australia. You must have misunderstood me."

"What was Nonno doing on the ship you were traveling on, was he a member of the crew?" Leah was getting a little impatient, especially when she realized that I was deliberately trying to keep them in suspense.

20

THE HELLENIC PRINCE

"As I said before, the Hellenic Prince was a raggedy old boat; for certain it had seen better days. I would never forget that tattered boat, though, because it had the precious cargo of the love of my life."

"When did you know that he was the love of your life?" asked Jane.

"You knew instantly, didn't you, Nonna? I think I heard you say that," said Leah.

"I don't think that's quite accurate."

"What do you mean, didn't you tell me that it was love at first sight?"

"Yes and no."

"Yes and no?" I could see that I had managed to confuse the girls.

"I think I'd better explain."

"I think you'd better!"

"I knew before I met him on that day on the Australia that something was about to take place. I was certain it would be a life-changing experience. If I was destined to meet the love of my life, I was certain I would recognize him. He would have adoring eyes.

His gentle touch would make me shiver. We would truly love each other categorically and unconditionally, not just for life, but also for all eternity. And strange as it may seem, he would be my equal."

"There was no equality between a man and a woman when you came to Australia," said Leah.

"No, there wasn't equality anywhere; many men treated a woman as an inferior factotum who had no mind of her own and had to be told what to do. This was another discrimination that had to be abolished. The time had come; we now lived in an era where we had realized that such barbarous and outdated practices were abominable. Hence, the man that I would consider spending my life with had to be my equal and my soul mate.

"Something was telling me that this was the man I was about to meet. Thus, when I saw him and he saw me, it was as if we recognized one another, as if we had known each other since always. I had heard of matches made in heaven, and now I had no doubt that ours was going to be a heavenly union. The question that I kept on asking myself was whether we would meet again. I told him I was going to Australia, but I had no idea which part of the globe he was traveling to. According to what Guido had told me, it was almost certain that the Hellenic Prince was headed for Australia.

"This, however, didn't tell me whether Michael was headed toward Australia. He could have been working on the boat, for all I knew. On the one hand I feared that we would never meet again, and on the other, feeling certain that we were meant to be together, we would, somehow find one another. Where or when, I had no idea.

"Since I didn't even know his surname, there was no way I could begin to look for him, let alone find him. And yet I never gave up hope. I remembered his gentle smile and his beautiful eyes and prayed that one day soon I would gaze into them once again, and this time it would be forever."

21

THE ROOFTOP

"Nonna, you are keeping us in suspense!" exclaimed Jane.

"Let Nonna tell the story," admonished Leah.

"Our two-room house with a shared kitchen was situated behind a fairly tall building—a kind of a boarding house where young men lived. I found out that the boats full of migrants, mainly men, who had emigrated either for work or for a sense of adventure, had arrived in town. Many of them were living in the tall building. Many times, as I went through the lane to go to the back where we lived, I would see many men climbing the external steps to go up to their rooms. Of course, as I went past, I would receive the so-called wolf whistle, which nauseated me."

"One morning my family went shopping, and I was left home with Nonna, who was in the kitchen waiting for her turn to start cooking lunch. Unexpectedly, I heard a beautiful voice singing the latest Italian song. I remember distinctly this feeling of expectation, the same as I had felt before I had seen Michael for the first time. Could the person singing possibly be him? Could this be an intuition or some crazy Sicilian premonition? Yet my intuition or sixth sense had served me well the first time, and my body was telling me once again that Michael was nearby. Without thinking, because if I had thought about it and my parents had found out, I would, in the very least have been slaughtered, I climbed on top of the roof of our house. I thought that from there I could spy a little and see who the singer was.

"The building being about three stories high, I could see just a head of someone under a shower. Was it Michael?

"I could not tell by the wet head of the person singing under the shower, but something deep within me was telling me that it was he. I heard voices, and I could see that my family was returning. I could not let my parents see me on the roof of the house or else I would be questioned and condemned on the spot without a jury and without listening to my defense. I quickly descended. Coming down from a roof and hanging from the gutter was somewhat precarious, to say the least. But since I could hear my family approaching, I jumped to the ground. I realized later that I could have broken my neck, but the vision of someone singing while taking a shower—and that that someone could have been Michael—made it worthwhile.   " W a s the person I had seen Michael? I hoped so. I would somehow find out the next day. But that night my father had an unpleasant surprise for us, but most especially for me."

22

TREACHEROUS FATE

"What happened, Nonna"? The girls demanded to know.

"That night at dinner, my father announced that he had found a larger house, and we were going to move over the weekend. The two-day holiday would give us the time to carry out our relocation. Once again, if it was Michael I had seen, I was going to be hauled away from him. It appeared to me that while we were chosen to be together, people did their very best to drag us apart. But I had news for them. If Michael was anywhere in this town, regardless of what my parents or anybody else would say, I would find him.

"How would I look for him, though? According to my father, the house where we were going to live was some distance away from the town, and we had no car. I had a bicycle, though, which was a gift from a friend. He had promised that he would give me the bicycle as soon as I learned to speak English. In his opinion, I had surpassed his knowledge of the language, which wasn't much, and for my birthday, he had given me the bicycle. I rode it everywhere— it gave me a sense of freedom. It also gave me the opportunity to look around the streets for Michael.

"We moved to the bigger house. It wasn't much, and the owner —a crotchety, draconian old man and his half-witted son— inhabited part of it. At least, though, we had a bedroom each. Of course, I would have preferred to live closer to town to see whether the head of the person I had spotted through a window having a shower really belonged to Michael. While my sixth sense was telling me that it was, my reason was asserting the contrary. My internal dialogue kept on telling me that Michael was breathing the same air as I was, but at the same time, I thought it was too good to be true.

"One Saturday morning, I had gone to town with my sister with the excuse to check in the post office box for any mail and to post some letters. The street was full of people because all the farmers had come to town to do their shopping, plus hundreds of young Italian immigrants, mainly men, crowded the place. Suddenly, as I looked in the crowd, I saw him . There was no mistaking it; Michael lived in the same town as I did. I was elated, overjoyed, and euphoric. Had he seen me? And if he had, would he recognize me?

"In a split second, so many questions were going through my mind. He did not look as if he had seen me. He must see me! I could not let him escape without seeing me. I would have to attract his attention somehow, but how? Good girls did not approach men in those days—it simply wasn't done. They waited like idiots for the man to make the first move. I was frenetic; he probably had forgotten all about me, anyhow. Maybe I read too much into our first encounter. He probably had a girlfriend, a fiancée, or a wife somewhere. My mind was in utter chaos. He didn't seem as if he were married. But then how would I know how married people looked? Did they look different? I had not actually taken much notice before.

"I was just about to walk away because I had totally convinced myself that he didn't feel the same way as I did, after all. If he had he would have felt my presence, he would somehow know that I was there. I looked toward him once again, and this time our eyes met. I was sure that he felt the way I did. The same sensation that I had felt on the Australia swathed me."

"Marianna?" He called out my name in a gentle tone.

"Michael!" I replied. I could hardly pronounce his name. I was so nervous and anxious.

"Actually, girls," I said to Leah and Jane, "I am just as overwhelmed now while I am narrating my love story."

I stopped to take hold of my emotions, but the girls urged me to continue.

"You are not thinking of stopping now in the middle of the story, are you?" they said.

"No, I shall continue, but reliving those moments brings back very emotional memories.

"In the crowd we lost sight of one another once again. His friends insisted that they could not stop to look at pretty girls; there would be plenty of time for that; now they had to rush to an appointment or else they would be late. Once more fate was trying to divide us, but this time it was different. Now, at least, we were not too distant from one another and surely it was a matter of time before we found each other again. I knew, at least, that he had not forgotten me, and the look in his eyes clearly spoke of love. I was sure of it."

"Who was that young man who called you by your name?" asked my sister.

"The man I am going to marry!" I replied. My sister looked at me as if I were crazy. Perhaps I was.

"How do you know him?"

"It's a long story. I will tell you later." For the moment I wanted to savor the joyous feeling of having found my love. Who could have imagined that he would have ended up in the same place as I was? He could have gone to the other side of the country, in which case we would have never found one another. I shivered at the thought. I realized also that our journey would not be easy. If we would decide to spend our lives together, I had my family to contend with. But as they say in many ways, love will find the way, love conquers all, and love moves mountains. However, who ever said those things, of course, did not know my parents."

23

HOT CHRISTMAS

Christmas was approaching, a somewhat different Christmas from any we had ever known. We were accustomed to flakes of snow and early morning church. Nine days before Christmas, we would get up early to get ready for the novena, which started at about four o'clock in the morning. The people who lived down the valley would awaken us. They would sing carols accompanied by bagpipes. As they walked past our homes, we would join them in a long procession. It was extremely cold, and the falling snow made the countryside a beautiful postcard. In the darkness of the early morning, young people touched hands and fell in love.

Nonna used to say to me that if one did not believe in God, he or she only had to look at the snowflakes, all different and all perfect —the faultless beauty of a creator. In those days we had no doubts or uncertainties, and we were happy and felt warm.

Christmas in Australia, however, brought with it doubts and uncertainties. The weather was hot, but many hearts were cold. I was of the opinion, though, that one day things would change, and the heat of the country would eventually create warm hearts.

Perhaps Michael and I would lightly touch hands this Christmas—the seal of our love we already felt in our hearts. What a miracle that would be! But where would I see Michael this Christmas? I was certain I would see him soon, though.

The Christmas planning had started. In Sicily we started the preparations weeks before, and I could see that here was no exception. Of course, we could not have the banquet to which we were accustomed, as we did not have many friends here, but we would have to have a banquet, nevertheless. The shopping had started and soon the cooking had begun. All those sweets that could be made ahead of time were already filling the street with a wonderful smell. I think people were getting to know us by the aromas emanating from our kitchen.

Yet my heart was full of sadness. I had hoped to spot Michael even from a distance, but since that day we saw one another, he was nowhere to be seen. I wondered why he had not made the effort to see me. He must know that I could not go to look for him. He would be working during the day, and at night it was impossible for me to go anywhere.

Christmas had arrived, but no flakes of snow were to be seen. Instead, the morning was brilliant with a magical golden light. We already could tell that we had a sweltering day ahead of us. Nevertheless, Christmas was a precious celebration no matter what the weather was or the country the festivity occurred in.

The previous night I had heard Papà telling Mother that he had invited a few friends from work for Christmas lunch. I had not taken much notice, because if it wasn't Michael, I wasn't interested in anyone else. There always would be friends or freeloaders who were willing to share a good meal with us.

After church, we rushed home. I was putting the final touches to the Christmas dinner table, when there was a knock at the door. My father went to answer it, while I continued to do the task at hand. Mother urged me on: "Hurry up, Marianna; we have guests at the door." I was about to tell her that I wasn't too interested, when the person who entered the dining room totally changed my somewhat despondent mood into total ecstasy. I was having a glimpse of heaven, I was sure. When my father introduced Michael to me, and as I shook his hand and he pronounced my name, I was aware that whether there was snow or heat, whether I was in my homeland or in my adopted country, nothing mattered, for as far as we were concerned, we were alone in the whole universe.

I had heard many times that miracles happen and especially at Christmas. Meeting Michael in my own home was, indeed, my Christmas miracle. I remembered how tedious and painful I had thought the banquets in Casa Del Feo were, but now I wished this would go on forever. Michael was sitting across the table from me and many times I felt his gaze upon me. My father talked about Michael and how they had met and, if I understood correctly, they worked together.

My father was telling Michael that he should settle down and get married. I was listening with interest to my father's conversation urging Michael to take a bride, but suddenly I realized that I was not the bride; it was someone else. Becoming conscious that he was telling him that that pretty girl they had seen the other day would make him a good wife, I became livid. I felt like throwing the centerpiece on the table at him, directly on his head. How dare he! Did he want to ruin my life? I thought. In all reality, though, my father had no idea that Michael and I knew each other, let alone were in love with one another. However, his knowledge or the lack of it would not make any difference. He would never agree to my having anything to do with Michael. But I will find the way, I told myself. After all, my father wasn't as big as the proverbial mountain.

"Didn't your sister know that the two of you knew one another?" inquired Leah.

"Yes, she did, but I was hoping she would not say anything."

"Did she … did she say anything?" asked Jane.

"No, she didn't."

During the meal, it was my mother who asked Michael when he had arrived in Australia and on which boat he had traveled.

"I came about the same time as you and your family did. The boat I came with was called Hellenic Prince. It was a very old boat, and it could not be compared with the Australia."

While Michael was talking about the boats, he was glancing at me. I hoped he would not say anything about our meeting. There would be plenty of time later for that, I thought.

"If you came the same time as my family," asked Papà, "how come you haven't been in this town for long? Did you go somewhere else before you came here?"

"Yes, I did. I had to go to a holding center."

"What is a holding center, and why did you have to go there?" asked Papà.

"It depended on ethnicity where migrants would be sent. British migrants were permitted to remain in the metropolitan area, and other European-assisted migrants were sent to Northam or Cunderdin. Northam, where I was sent, was an army camp converted as an accommodation center for us."

"You were a government-assisted migrant, Michael?" I wished my father would not continue with the questioning.

"Yes, I was. Many young people were enticed by propaganda posters, which represented Australia as a rich country with flourishing industry where there was plenty of opportunity and employment for everyone. In a time of unrest in Europe, you can understand how attractive that seemed to all the young men. So, thousands signed up to migrate. Of course, your situation is relatively different," said Michael.

"Yes," replied Papà. Relatives nominated most of the Sicilian people, and since the government did not assist them, they paid their own expenses for the trip over to Australia. I was sponsored by relatives in Queensland, so I went to live with them until I transferred to Western Australia."

"What made you come to Western Australia?"

"Some family matters, which had to be sorted out before I could sponsor my own family," responded Papà, waving his hand to show that he did not want to discuss our private family matters.

Nonna had been silent up to now, but I could see she liked him. Whether she liked him for me was a different matter. She later said,

"What a nice young man. He has the hands of a writer." I had no idea what the hands of a writer were supposed to look like, but I did not comment on it and left it at that, assuming that he had nice hands.

We decided that seeing that it was a beautiful day, or better still my father and mother decided, to have coffee outside on the back veranda. There was quite a bit of arranging to be done, so Michael offered to help. While everyone was each doing his or her own thing, Michael and I had a brief moment alone. I was amazed at the fact that something like that was allowed to happen, but I was grateful that it did. Michael and I were actually able to exchange a few words.

"I had no idea that you were the daughter of my friend and that I would find you on Christmas Day," said Michael, looking around, making sure that no one would see or hear him.

"Nor I," I replied softly.

"It was a wonderful surprise. I have been asking about you, but not knowing your surname, it was impossible to find you—no one seemed to know where you lived. Finally, I know your full name, where you come from, and where you live," said Michael, smiling with happiness.

"I don't know anything about you either, except your name—actually, I still don't.

"One day soon we will be able to really talk and get to know one another. I'm afraid, though that your father will not allow you to see me. It seems that he doesn't even think that we could ever be together." I could hear the sadness in Michael's voice.

Before I could reply, the clamor of voices and the rattling of dishes were getting closer to us. Obviously, my family had not noticed that we were alone, otherwise it would not have happened. I was grateful for the few words we were able to exchange.

Before the throng could get to us, Michael quickly touched my hand and whispered: "You must know by now, Marianna, that I'm in love with you."

"I love you too," I replied timidly. I was so happy.

24

LOVE IN HIGH PLACES

My family had suddenly descended and erupted on us like the volcano Etna, and that was that. The chatter continued, but now, cradled with Michael's love, I felt courageous and certain that we would find the way to be together. It was my father who inadvertently gave us the opportunity to encounter one another.

"Did you know, Michael, that I'm building a family home?" my father asked.

"Yes," replied Michael, "you told me. When will it be finished?"

"Not for a while yet. In a few weeks' time, it will be ready for the construction of the roof. It will have to be done on the weekend because I can't leave work."

"Can I help?" asked Michael.

"Yes, thank you. I would appreciate that."

So, this was what was going to happen next, I told myself.

I decided that Michael and I were going to meet on the roof of the house. All the tree climbing I had done in Sicily was going to come in handy. A roof of a house was nothing in comparison to a very tall poplar tree that was swaying in the wind. Given that no one was around, I could have a conversation with Michael on the roof of our new house. I just had to pray that my father would be absent for some time.

As I had done many times in Sicily, I was hoping that I would be asked to take either morning coffee or lunch or both to the workmen. The more I thought about it, the more I became sure that it was going to happen. Of course, in order to prevent my family from guessing my plan, when asked I would pretend to be annoyed. This never failed to compel or even force them to make me do as I was told. This time, however, instead of being maneuvered, the subterfuge would be on them. I continued to plan my little escapade to perfection, and when I heard my father say that the house was ready for the roof, and that they would start on the following Saturday, I was ready to bring coffee and all the tasty goodies to the men at work.

"Marianna, you must take morning coffee to the workers at the new house this morning." The command came sharp and abrasive as the baronesses were used to in their homeland. They didn't realize that I was a grown young woman ready to commit my life to the person I loved with all my heart; not that I wanted them to know just yet. So I replied as expected.

"Why me? I had other plans this morning."

"Yes. You. Who else then?"

"Oh, OK then. If I must go."

"Yes, you must.

I was wearing a pretty dress but realized that if I had to climb on top of the roof, it would not look good. So I decided to wear a pair of slacks with a beautiful and flattering blouse. I got the basket, which I had helped to get ready by putting in a few little extras, tied it to my bicycle like I used to do with my horse, jumped on it, and off I went. As I got closer to the new house, my heart was pounding.

While I was telling the story, I noticed that both Leah and Jane were sitting looking at me without saying a word. "Girls," I said, "you look tired. Maybe we should leave my love story for another day."

"Don't you even think it! We want to hear it now," they both exclaimed.

"Where was I? Oh, yes. I was going to the new house to take coffee to Michael."

"And your father. Don't forget him. Yes, don't forget him," said the girls, urging me on.

As soon I arrived, I realized that the person on the roof was Michael, and my father was nowhere to be seen. I wondered where my father could be, but I was grateful for his absence. I could finally have a discussion with Michael without anyone's disapproving and stern stare.

Michael was on the roof, concentrating on the work at hand. He had not seen me; I climbed the ladder and slowly went toward him. When he saw me, his face lit up with a beautiful smile. "Marianna!" he said with joy and surprise in his voice. "What are you doing here?"

"I came to bring you coffee."

"I mean here on the roof. Be careful—here, let me hold you."

Since I liked the idea of being held by him, I did not mention that I was a good climber and that I had done it since I was a child. He held me tightly and then kissed me. What a moment that was. He looked around and he gently let me go. We had not realized that everyone who went past on the road would see us, and my father would soon find out. But I didn't care; he would have to know soon or later anyway. Remembering my father, I asked Michael where he was.

"He went to hardware shop to purchase nails and things needed for the roof," Michael said. "I'm glad, though, to have this time alone with you."

"So am I."

"There is something I want to ask you," continued Michael. "You know that I have loved you since the first time we met on the ship."

"So have I."

"Will you marry me, Marianna?"

I looked into his eyes and replied, "Yes, I will marry you."

Then, as if regaining consciousness, I said, "Let's go down before someone sees us. Before my father comes back, we can talk while we have coffee."

While I was pouring the coffee, Michael said, "You have made me the happiest man in the world."

"Before we can make any plans for the future, as tradition demands, you have to ask my parents for my hand in marriage."

"I know, but I am worried about their reaction. It is obvious that while I am acceptable to them as a friend, they are not even remotely thinking of me as a future son-in-law. You heard your father telling me to marry another girl?"

"I know. He thinks of me as a young girl and not as a young woman ready for marriage."

"You are young," acquiesced Michael gently.

"Age has nothing to do with it. Seeing that we are in love, marriage is the next sensible step to take."

"You think your parents will eventually approve."

"You ask them and leave the rest to me. I will convince them that you are the man for me—the man of my dreams."

Michael was just about to embrace me once again when we spotted Papà coming around the corner. As he whispered, "I will see you soon," I quickly reassured him once again and made myself busy with the coffee percolator. When my father arrived, he was none the wiser about what had just happened.

25

CONFRONTATION

One evening when Papà came home from work, I heard him say to Mamma that Michael wanted to come and have a talk with them.

"What does he want?"

My father shrugged his shoulders and replied: "I haven't any idea." I looked away in case they would guess that my heart was pounding.

"When is he coming?" inquired my mother.

"Tomorrow night! I invited him to dinner."

"Haven't you any idea of what he could possibly want?"

"No," said Papà pensively. "Perhaps he has found a girl, and he wants to tell us."

"He is close," I thought.

"If that were the case, he would tell you. He would not want to come and discuss it with me. I hardly know him. I have only seen him a few times." My mother had a puzzled look.

"We will know soon enough," replied my father with a dismissive tone in his voice.

I was nervous and I tossed and turned most of the night. When I finally fell asleep, I dreamed of Michael. We were sitting under a tree, holding hands and making plans for our future together. During the day I kept on praying that God would give me the right words to convince my parents that Michael was the right person for me and that I loved him with all my heart.

Dinner was being prepared with the usual lavishness that was customary in our home. While my grandmother and my mother were cooking dinner, I was asked to set the table. I did that with meticulous attention to detail. Everything looked perfect except me. I needed to change and look beautiful for Michael. I tried on different dresses, but none of them seemed suitable. I finally decided to wear a pretty silk floral dress.

My mother called me to hurry up because our guest was about to arrive, and "things" were not yet ready. She usually panicked when she had visitors, but this evening I was also panicking; I was worried in case we had forgotten something. Suddenly there was a knock at the door. Everyone was coming in and out of the kitchen and since no one was going to open the door, whether they liked it or not, it seemed that I was the one elected to let our visitor in. Not that I minded, of course, but if they knew the reason why Michael was coming, I most definitely would not be allowed to do so.

My mother would say that it wasn't proper for me to greet the guest. But greet the guest I did. Not the greeting I would have liked to give, of course, but under the circumstances there was no way I could throw my arms around Michael's neck and get away with it. I gave my hand instead, and he squeezed it and quickly kissed it. That was enough, however, to send me to the highest heaven.

While dinner was served everybody's eyes were on Michael. I felt sorry for the poor darling, and I would not have blamed him if he had taken off and run for his life, never to be seen again in our home. I know I wanted to run away. After dinner, coffee was served. I could see that my father was becoming anxious or better still curious to know what Michael could possibly want from him. Not to mention the rest of the family since no one had any intention to stop staring and bring to a halt their hovering over Michael. Poor, poor love!

"Michael, you were going to ask me something?" Like what seemed a thunderous bolt, the question had come out from my father's mouth. I jumped, and I am sure Michael did also.

"Yes," uttered Michael. We had reached the point of no return, and soon my father's wrath would be audible and felt by everyone in the room. Hopefully I was exaggerating, but I very much doubted it. I was sure, though, that he would be kind to Michael since he appeared to like him.

"You know you can ask me anything."

"Ah ... ahh ... ahhh!" I wished I could have laughed out aloud. Michael, however, must have believed him because he continued. "The other day you told me that I should find a girl and get married."

"Yes, I remember. Have you found someone you like?" Father's voice seemed relaxed and somewhat relieved.

"Yes, I have. We fell in love the first time we met."

"Oh, yes, love at first sight. I am told that happens sometimes. Are you sure, Michael, that it is love and not just some sort of infatuation? You know, Michael, that I want the best for you. You have become a very dear friend to me." You could tell that father spoke from the heart.

"It's definitely love. The kind of love that lasts a lifetime." Michael sounded emotional and I could hardly hold back my tears.

"Who is she? Do I know her?" inquired Papà.

"Indeed, you do. You know her very well. It is your beautiful daughter, Marianna. I would like the honor of her hand in marriage."

"My daughter?" There was a loud bang of pots and pans as they hit the floor. My father's mouth was still open. "My daughter? My daughter Marianna? You know what you are asking, and if I were to allow it, do you know what you are in for? First of all, she is far too young for marriage, and I doubt it if she knows what love is. Second, she can't cook; she is totally absorbed in books because she wants to study and go to university. This, of course, cannot happen since she will never have the appropriate language for tertiary studies. However, she continues to dream. All in all, I will have to be honest with you. She will not make you a good wife."

I expected a list as to why Michael and I should not be married from my father, but this was ridiculous. Yes, I wanted to study, but I had also realized that my dream, due to my being less than fluent in the English language, could not come true.

As for cooking, I had spent many hours watching Carmela back in Sicily and Nonna here in Australia. I had seen the wonderful dishes they could produce, and I knew I could do the same, if not better. My father had never taken an interest in what was considered woman's work so he would have no way of knowing—absolutely no idea as to what I could do. I expected my mother to come to my rescue, but she would not contradict him in front of a stranger. I was humiliated, to say the least. It was Michael's reply that made my resentment subside.

"I love Marianna and I am certain she loves me." He was looking directly at me when he asserted my love for him; I nodded to reassure him of my profound love. "As for studying," he continued, "if and when she is ready to do so, I will totally support her wishes, you have my word on that. And what was the other thing she cannot do? Oh yes, cooking! We don't have to worry about that since I can cook. Before I left Italy, I made sure I learned to cook the essentials. I can make a good sauce for pasta; I can make a pizza and grill a steak, so rest assured that we will not starve. I know Marianna is young, but people are getting married fairly young these days."

To my father's list of my uselessness and unreserved and complete worthlessness, Michael had answered with absolute love and trust in me. Nothing mattered to him except our love. My father wasn't convinced though, and he had something else to add to the list of the things I could not do. According to him, I wasn't able to feel any sort of emotion.

"My daughter does not know what love is, therefore, she cannot feel or be in love with you." Now he had gone too far. So, this was his opinion of me—his own daughter? Many times, people had told me that I was a fairly intelligent person and now I had become useless and heartless. I had news for him—he was the one who was heartless.

"I do so!" I replied assertively.

"You do what?" There was anger in his voice for my daring to involve myself in a conversation that according to him was not of my concern.

"I do love Michael."

"You don't even know Michael."

"Yes, I do." I could see that my mother and grandmother were scared for me. I on the other hand, was not going to be frightened by him anymore.

"I do know Michael. We met on the boat on the way to Australia."

"How could that happen? You were traveling on different ships."

"We met anyway." He looked at my mother, silently asking her if she knew about this. My mother, like a good Sicilian, lifted her shoulders to her ears, which meant no sacciu (I don't know).

My father then turned to Michael and apologetically said, "I wish I had known about this before you came—I wish my daughter had told me so I could have been prepared." Once again, I was completely at fault. No matter what I did and said, my father was going to punish me for my indiscretion of having fallen in love.

"Please do not blame Marianna. If anybody is at fault it is I." Michael looked sad. My father suddenly realized that he was supposed to be a gentleman and said, "I do apologize, Michael, I was caught unaware."

"No need to apologize; just give me the permission and the honor of marrying Marianna."

"Of course, you deserve an answer, and I will give it to you. However, I need some time. I need to speak to my daughter first. As soon as I have done that, I shall respond to your request."

The drill, the grill and the probing will now commence, I thought, but there was nothing that my father could say or do to me to make me change my mind. He somehow had to understand that Michael and I were meant for each other. When Michael excused himself and said his goodbyes, he shook my hand. To reassure him, I whispered that everything was going to be all right.

26

THE GRILL

"Marianna, come into my room. I want to talk to you!" My father's roaring voice shook the fragile home to its foundation. I could see that my mother, my grandmother, and my sister were terrified for me. They probably thought he was going to kill me. I followed him into his room and mother slithered after me. My father looked at me, or should I say glared at me.

"Do you realize what you have done?"

"What have I done? I haven't done anything yet."

"Don't talk to your father like that." I could see that my mother was trying to ingratiate herself to her husband to calm him down. Every time she was scared, she would grovel to him. And she was frightened now of what he might do, so she tried to pacify him by stroking his hand.

"You should have come to me first."

"If I had, you would have told me that Michael should come and ask you, and that is exactly what he did—he has asked you. I can't see why it is a problem."

"You don't see a problem?" he shrieked, pulling his hand away from his wife.

"No, I don't. Why would my falling in love with a wonderful man be a problem? People have been doing it since the world began."

"Yes, they have. But I am not worried about the world—I am worried about you. I don't think you know what love is."

"Yes. I do. I knew the instant I met Michael. I knew that if I didn't marry him, I would not marry anybody else. And marry him I will, with or without your consent."

"You can't marry him without my consent, you're underage. So if I refuse to consent, there will be no wedding."

"Well in that case, there is only one option for me to take." By now my tears were desperately trying to appear and the lump in my throat was about to choke me. But I must not cry in front of my father; he would think that was a weakness.

"I am glad you are coming to your senses. You realize that your only option is to obey me and forget all about Michael. I feel sorry for Michael, though, because he is a good person and a great friend." My father was admitting he liked Michael, but not enough to allow him to become my husband? This was ludicrous.

"My forgetting about Michael was not the option I meant. I could never do that. What I meant was that if you will not consent to us marrying, then we will have to elope. After we do that, you will give your consent to save face. Isn't that what happens in Sicily?"

My father's face was livid. He had not bargained for this, but I wasn't going to allow him to destroy my life. I had been through too much in my young life, things that probably he wasn't even aware of, not to know the importance of truly loving someone and spending my life with him.

"You wouldn't, Marianna. Only people from the lower class did that in Sicily and not a well-to-do young lady like you."

"There is no question about it. I would do it. Anyway, we are in Australia, now not in Sicily, and in all probability we are the lower class here. Or haven't you noticed? I think I have said everything I have to say, and now it is up to you to find out what your preference is between my eloping and your consent," I said as I walked out of the room, leaving mother trying to placate him by telling him that this was a horrible world we lived in, and how the young people of today had no respect for the adults. Of course, she did not realize that this was a recurrent theme that had been used throughout the ages, and it would continue to be used by people like them shunned all responsibility. Everything negative that happened was always somebody else's fault.

I was angry, and as usual my brain had gone into an accelerated mode where the past and present became fused. I went to bed that night and sobbed for hours. Tomorrow it would be another battle, another heartache reinforced by attacks on my lack of discernment, lack of proper etiquette, and the lack of prudence. But I would not be swayed. I had gone too far to turn back now. I must admit I was surprised at my own ability to defy my father. I never thought I could have been able to do that. I certainly had never done it before. By my unusual behavior he should have realized how much I loved Michael and that there wasn't anything I would not do for him. I most definitely would not compromise the love of a lifetime.

The following day, to my surprise, none of those things that I feared happened. I think my parents had realized that I wasn't giving them ultimatums for the sake of it, but because we were serious about the love Michael and I felt for one another.

"So, you love Michael, and he loves you," Papà said, his voice a little more subdued than the previous evening.

"Are you sure, Marianna?" inquired Mamma.

"Of course, I am sure. I think I have made it abundantly clear." I glanced toward Nonna, and she had a slight smile while she winked at me. It appeared that at least one member of my family was on my side. I knew that Nonna liked Michael; she had said so the first time he came to our home. Come to think of it, everybody liked him. It was me they weren't too sure about.

"I have a proposition to make to you."

"A proposition?"

"Yes, don't look so shocked, Marianna. After all we want the best for you," said Father, and Mother nodded.

"Michael is the best for me and I for him."

"So you say. But it's our duty to make sure that it is the case."

"How are you going to do that?"

"We have decided that we are going to give you two months for you both to get to know each other.

"How do we do that?" I was relaxing a little.

"Michael can come to see you at home, and you can go out with him as long as you're accompanied by someone from the family." I was sure that what he was proposing was the best I was going to receive, so I agreed.

"After the two months are over, I will ask you if you still want to go ahead with the engagement and then the wedding. If you still feel the same as you do now, then we will consent and give you our blessing."

I felt like jumping and shouting for joy. We must not forget, though, that the English had been in the Mediterranean looking after Sicily for a long time, and we Sicilians had adopted a few of their mannerisms, one of which was not showing one's feelings publicly. So, after hugging and thanking my mother and father, I went into my room and jumped and shouted for joy. No doubt, my family, not to mention people going past in the street, heard me.

27

A BEAUTIFUL LOVE STORY

Leah and Jane had listened to the narrative of my love story. They had been listening for hours without being even remotely bored. I would have thought that their interest would have diminished by now. And yet they pleaded for more.

"What a beautiful love story, Nonna! Please don't stop now. Please, please continue."

"Aren't you tired? I certainly am. I have been talking for hours. Can't we continue another day?" Reluctantly they agreed with the promise that the narration would continue the next day.

"I promise," I said.

My family was coming for dinner, so I had to start the cooking. I went into the kitchen, but already the beautiful fragrance of the tomato sauce was filling the house, and the ambience was almost like that of long ago. As I entered the kitchen, my husband greeted me in his usual way.

"Ciao, bella."

"Ciao, amore. I was coming to cook, but as I can see, everything is almost ready."

"I heard you talking with the girls. You were all so engrossed that I decided to start dinner.

"Thank you for doing that. I lost track of time. I always do that when I talk with Leah and Jane."

"I know it is easy to do. They are beautiful girls and there is nothing you would not do for them. They adore their nonna."

"And their nonno," I responded.

Smiling, he said, "The feeling is definitely mutual." Changing the subject, he asked, "Who is coming for dinner tonight?"

"Everyone is."

"Where are the girls now?"

"I left them in the study. They are doing their work on the computer."

"You are going to continue your narration tomorrow?"

"Yes, I promised I would. They are very inquisitive. They want to know every detail of our past."

"Didn't you tell me that your nonna did the same for you?"

"Yes, I did. I was very inquisitive too."

"I know, you still are. It is the dilemma of intelligent people," he said, smiling.

"So, you think I am intelligent?"

"You know I do. Haven't I told you many times?"

"Yes, you have." I replied, while throwing my arms around his neck and kissing him. This was how our daughters and their husbands found us.

"These two are always in each other's arms," said Natalie.

"Yes," admitted Marie Teresa. "One wonders how they get things done."

"We do though. As you can see, dinner is ready." I replied.

"Yes, we could smell it down the street," acknowledged our sons-in-law. "We are starved."

"Where are the girls?" inquired Natalie.

"They're in my study, working on the computer."

"I will call them to dinner."

"Please do."

It was always a joyful occasion having the family for dinner. It reminded me of the times gone by when Donna Camilla, my dearest nonna, and Donna Eleonora, my mother, were the two ladies who had hosted many banquets. Everyone back in Sicily respected them and once people had come to know them, they were also well esteemed here in Australia.

I missed them so much, but they would live on through me. I was the oldest, and as such, I felt I had the duty to make the rich legacy live on, first through me and through my progeny. Cooking had always been one of my passions, and I could already see that my family was inheriting my dedication.

"Bella!"

"Yes?" I quickly responded to being called "Bella" as if it were my real name.

"I had an idea."

"So did I," I replied. It would not surprise me if we had thought the same thing at the same time. It happened so often, which proved that we were indeed kindred spirits.

"I am sure we have had the same idea. Tell me your idea."

"No, you go first." The voices that were getting close to the dining room prevented us from voicing our idea. It was not until later, after the family had gone home, that we picked up our early discussion. Before departing, the girls made me promise that the following day I would resume the narrative of the story of my life.

They were so anxious to learn all their ancestral roots. Actually, they were no different from how I was at their age. I too had insisted to be told all about the family. I, however, except for the good and romantic parts of my family's history, had to find out the hidden mysteries by myself. There was no way that my mother or grandmother would reveal those secrets, which according to them should remain buried forever.

"What was your idea?" I asked.

"I thought it would be nice if we went to Italy with the family. The girls would enjoy your showing them Sicily. That would give them a better understanding of the family and their place of origin."

"Exactly what I had in mind." There was joy in my heart.

"Next time they come we will discuss the possibility of all of us taking the trip. Perhaps, it could happen the next vacation that they have."

The following day Leah and Jane, as if they had sensed what we had discussed, started to talk about Sicily.

"Nonna, how many times have you been back to Sicily?"

"Twice. Once when your auntie and your mother were young girls, and another time Nonno and I went."

"Did you like it?"

"Yes."

"Was it the way you remembered it?"

"The beauty of the island had not changed, but everything that was dear to me had. In a sense it was like visiting a strange place."

"Were your aunts still alive?" asked Leah.

"Yes, they were, but the people, my dearest friends, those people who had been instrumental in shaping my life were not. I missed them so much. It was too painful, and at the time I could not deal with the memories." I had to change the subject soon, I thought, or else the girls would see the tears that were starting to appear in my eyes. I turned around so that the girls would not see me crying and changed the subject.

"Do you want something to eat?" I asked.

"Some of your biscotti will be nice," they replied.

We shared the coffee and latte with my famous biscotti and chatted about their ambitions for their future. As soon as we had finished and the dishes had been washed and put away, I was ushered into the study.

"Please continue your story," they both pleaded.

"OK!" I replied. "Where were we? I don't remember where we left off."

"Stop teasing, you do so remember," said Leah, and Jane agreed. "Anyway, you left the story where your father gave you a period of two months to prove to them that you were really in love."

"Oh, yes. Now I remember."

And so it was. Michael was told that he could come to our home to get to know me. We were both over the moon about the decision. We were certain that we would pass the test and soon we would be husband and wife. Occasionally, when we thought no one was watching, we would hold hands or steal a little kiss. When we were allowed to go out, we went to see a film, accompanied by my sister or grandmother. We had little chance for in-depth conversation, but we did not care about that because we felt we had always known one another.

When the two months were up, my father wanted to speak to both of us. He asked me whether my feelings were the same toward Michael.

"No!" I replied.

My father looked almost pleased, and Michael seemed shattered, but at the same time there was a glimpse of disbelief. I suddenly realized that I had been misunderstood and quickly said.

"What I meant was that no, my feelings are not the same as they were two months ago. but they have intensified a hundredfold. I love Michael more than life itself and cannot wait until the day we are husband and wife." Michael breathed a sigh of relief, and my father looked somewhat disappointed.

Still hoping, my father asked, "What about you, Michael?"

"I feel the same as Marianna, and my promise is that I will do everything in my power to make her happy for the rest of our lives."

My father reminded Michael what a useless wife I would be, and how he would find me reading a book instead of doing my housework. He should not be blamed for my lack of domestic proficiency. According to him, he had tried to bring me up in the right way, but unfortunately, he seemed to have failed.

My nonna tried to intervene by coming to my defense. I guessed what she was about to say. She would say to my father that contrary to what he thought of me, I was a good cook. I signaled her not to say anything. What I could or could not do was not important because first, there was nothing she could say that would convince my father, and second, I had the will power and the ability to learn. The love Michael and I felt for each other was the most wonderful thing that would keep us together forever.

After the so-called reluctant blessing we received, the preparation for our engagement started. In Sicily we have a color for every occasion. For the bride, of course it was virginal white; for the birth of a boy, it was blue; for a birth of a girl, it was pink; for a university graduate, it was red; and for an engagement, it was green.

Now that my family had decided to accept Michael as my future husband, as usual they became irrational with the preparation of the engagement party. Since they thought everything should be green, they went in search of everything green. I suggested that we could save the money for green tablecloths and green decorations by having the celebration outside in the backyard where the grass was perfectly cut and green. Of course, I was given the usual look that was awarded to a young idiot who knew nothing of such matters. When they tried to find the usual green sugared almonds to place in little green bags to give to people, my mother looked disgusted. What she could find in Australia were little jars of sugared almonds all in different colors. What was a travesty of misrepresentation and probably considered uncivilized was the fact among the pink and blue sugared almonds there were yellow ones, and no one knew which occasion they were suited for. I suggested they were simply for eating and again I was given that "unclean" look not wanting to offend anyone by calling it a dirty look.

The green sugared almonds were not to be found anywhere. That, translated by superstitious Sicilians, meant that if the color of hope were not to be found, my married life would be hopeless. So, the engagement was postponed for a few weeks in order to send away for the elusive green sugared almonds, which were not eaten but placed on show in a cup in the china cabinet, never to be touched again, or at least not until they were attacked by tiny creatures and had to be thrown away.

I did not mind the delay because whether I had a ring on my finger or not, it did not alter the fact that soon I was going to be Michael's wife. While I was talking, I noticed that the girls were trying not to laugh. So, I said:

"You think it's funny? You should have been there to see those ladies: my mother and grandmother surrounded by everything green and thinking they were doing the very best for me."

The girls could not ignore any longer the hilarity of the situation and burst into an unbridled laughter. Of course, I laughed too. When the amusement had subsided, I said: "Wait, there is more."

"More?"

"Yes, there is definitely more."

"Please continue, Nonna."

"While we were waiting for the green sugared almonds to arrive, my dress was being made. The material was of a beautiful organza. And guess what color it was?"

Both Leah and Jane laughing, said, "Green."

"Correct!"

Before the engagement, I was warned not to prolong the kissing at the exchange of the rings. I was not to make people talk and dishonor our family.

Before you ask, yes, according to my family, you could disgrace everyone by kissing your fiancé. Not to mention that I had a responsibility toward my sister who was not married. My behavior would affect her future. She would be judged by my behavior, not hers. I agreed to all the admonitions to keep the peace. After all, I would soon be Michael's wife, and then I could give him all the kisses I desired.

When the day of our engagement arrived, I got dressed and forgot that I blended in with the greenery. I was so happy because Michael had no eyes for anything or anybody except me. His beautiful smiling eyes told me of his immeasurable love. As we looked into each other's eyes, everything and everybody else disappeared. It was as if we were alone in the whole universe.

I was just about to throw my arms around his neck and give him the longest and the most passionate kiss, when I remembered that I had to give Michael a little peck to safeguard everyone's honor, since that was the thing which mattered most to Sicilians. They killed to protect their honor. I never understood that, but then again, there were many things I did not understand, and which left me perplexed. Much of the reasoning was a conundrum for many people.

The months went by, and my family kept on asking me if I was still sure of the enormous step we were about to undertake. I reassured them that I had never been as certain of anything else in my whole life.

"What about your studies? You wanted to study more than anything else in your life."

"Well, I realized that in life you couldn't have everything. It is obvious that with our coming to Australia, things have changed. I wasn't born here, so it would have been difficult to enter a tertiary institution."

"Michael keeps on telling us that you will make it one day."

"How can that be possible? I am getting married, and I will have children, so I can't see how I can attend school. Michael loves me, so he cannot see the unfeasibility of such a promise. Anyway, as years go by, the impossibility grows."

"Will you have any regrets?" asked Nonna.

"None!"

28

THE DREAM COMES TRUE

No! There would never be any regrets. No regrets of any kind. Our love was too great, and no matter what, it would last forever. Michael adored me, and I worshipped him. Yes, I wanted to study but since circumstances had prevented that, I would count my blessings in having found the love of my life. Being a migrant in a foreign land it was not easy to learn a language, but through tenacity and persistence, I had to come to understand and speak the language. As a result, I was able to understand the people of Australia. So, in many ways, this in itself was an enormous achievement.

"Nonna, tell us about the wedding," said the girls in unison.

"What is there to say about my wedding?"

As the date approached, my family became more frantic with the preparations. My wedding dress was being made by the dressmaker; invitations had to be worded perfectly. The list of the guests had to be made, which in my opinion was not difficult because my mother and grandmother wanted to invite the entire population of the town. I pointed out that I wanted a small wedding. They reassured me that the list of the guests included only those people who had invited us, and no one could be excluded. I did not argue because, according to my family, the only things that I had to be concerned with were to make a beautiful bride and to act composed and elegant.

"How many people were invited? asked Jane.

"According to my family, it would be a small wedding of two hundred and fifty people."

I like to stress that my family's concept of small was different from that of the rest of the world. I did not mind, however, because I was too happy to allow myself to be concerned too much with triviality. The hubbub, though, of many women who told the caterers what to do was unbearable. It was thought that the food they were serving was not nearly enough, so they decided that they would make trays, and trays, and trays of sweets. To achieve this enormous task, they invited most of our lady friends. They said they were honored, and about twenty, give or take a few, were all in the kitchen.

The hubbub now resembled World War II. I should know that, even if I were a very small child, the memory of it would never go away. I could not take it any longer, so I went into my room and read a book. I came out when the voices were complimenting themselves for a job well done. They said goodbye to me, and I said goodbye to them. They weren't even aware that I was missing from the scene. When I saw trays of sweets all over the house, I nearly lost my cool.

I could not lose my temper now. It would not be long. Once married to Michael, I would be my own person and my family would have to step aside and allow my husband and me to make our own decisions. Or would they? Meanwhile, Michael, who had just come in, was asked to take the trays of sweets to the caterers. When I saw the scene, I was about to break out in loud laughter, but with all my will power, quietly smiled instead. One must admit that things were back to front. It should have been the caterers to prepare food for us and not the other way around.

The day of our wedding dawned with a peaceful atmosphere and the dawn gave way to a brilliant sunshine. My heart was thumping with all sorts of emotions. My sister, who was going to be my bridesmaid, and I were getting ready. My mother came into the room and told me that I looked beautiful, gave me her blessings, and told me not to forget the talk that we had had the other evening. I said I would remember, but it hadn't been much of a talk.

She had told me that if I had contact with my husband, I would have a baby. I had read in books about sex but not in a specific sort of way. Nothing was specific in those days, so the mother usually explained the facts of life to the daughter. My mother had made me understand that tomorrow I would be pregnant. I must admit, this was one of my fears; perhaps I was too young to be a mother.

The wedding was beautiful, Michael was handsome, I felt beautiful, and the whole world was full of wonderful colors, and it was beautiful. Soon it was time for us to leave our reception. Michael and I were finally alone.

I stopped a little, thinking and remembering. Even though I was told I was quite intelligent, I realized how naive I had been on my wedding night. I kept on remembering my mother's words: if I had contact with my husband, the following day I would be pregnant.

"Nonna, please continue. Why are you hesitating? Tell us everything. Your wedding must have been beautiful," said Leah.

"I am a little embarrassed by the thoughts and fears I had on my wedding night. So many uncertainties, but perhaps I can tell you in a way that would not disclose all the intimate details. Everything is discussed openly these days anyway, which is good; honesty always is."

"You look embarrassed, Nonna." The girls gave me a hug.

"I am supposed to be the adult here. I shall continue without trying to be totally humiliated. Since my mother had told me that if I were intimate with my husband, I would have a baby. It stood to reason that if we were intimate twice, we would have twins. It was totally logical to me. I had to talk to my husband, and quickly, because I knew, that even though I could perhaps manage one child, two would be a different story.

"Eventually, I got the courage to talk to my husband about it. I told him that while I would be happy to have a child, twins were out of the question. At first, he did not understand what I was saying, but eventually when he did, he held me in his arms and told me what my mother should have told me. I felt mortified and totally embarrassed. My embarrassment was such that I felt like running away or putting my head under a pillow and staying there for the rest of my life. Eventually though, we managed to laugh, and we have laughed ever since." The girls were laughing now. At first it was a smile, and then it grew into a laugh and continued into uncontrollable laughter.

"Perhaps I should have left that little story unsaid. Maybe it should have stayed a secret with Nonno and me."

"No, Nonna, it's a beautiful story. It tells us how different things are now."

"Yes, I must admit, today there is more openness and truth. I can't really blame my mother for not telling me the facts of life. She probably did not know how to broach the subject. I knew how to make love, though; I just did not know the number of times one could indulge."

I looked at Leah and Jane and realized there was no stopping their laughter any time soon.

"So, as you know," I continued, "twelve months after Nonno I were married, we had our firstborn, a beautiful girl, your mother, and two years later we had the other gorgeous girl, your auntie." The laughter grew louder. I knew what my granddaughters were thinking. By now I felt a little uncomfortable, so I looked away, and as I smiled, I thought to myself, No, we made love more than twice.

29

THE UNBELIEVABLE AMBITION

I loved my family. Actually, there was nothing we each did that wasn't with the other person in mind. I heard once that if one wanted a marriage to succeed, one would have to give 100 percent to the other. I was young, but of one thing I was certain, I wanted to love and be loved with the same passion that Michael and I first had when we first met. So, I gave 100 percent, and I received the same and more in return.

Of course, our love grew and changed. It grew to the point that when our eyes met, we knew what the other was thinking. This was not just the kind of love that one had for a person in time, but it was almost a sacred timeless love. However, that passion I had for learning would never go away, so I decided that I would continue to learn with my children. As the children went to school, not only would I help them with their schoolwork, but they were helping me to learn.

Michael built a lovely home for us, and I thought that I had everything life could possibly offer. Natalie Eleonora and Marie Teresa were very intelligent children, and I tried to guide them toward university. At times, I thought, I was living a little of my life through them, and this was not the right thing to do. They should live their lives guided by their passions and not mine. Of course, I kept on telling myself an education was essential to get a good job and be treated with respect. As it was, they seemed to have an aptitude for learning, so I did not have to compel them to study toward university. So when the time came, their applications were accepted, and first Natalie and a few years later Marie Teresa entered university. My husband and I were so proud of the girls.

I will never forget the day that Natalie was accepted at university. We were anxiously waiting for the postman to arrive and when he did, Natalie ran out to grab the letter from him. I was almost certain that he had handed two letters to her, but when I only saw one in her hands, I thought I had made a mistake. We were so excited about her wonderful results. I told her that I would call the family to celebrate her achievements that night.

When Michael came home from work, I saw him talking to Natalie. I thought he was congratulating her. It wasn't until later that I realized what the secrecy was all about. He called all of us together and took a letter out of his pocket. As he started to talk, I didn't comprehend why he was saying something about a promise he had made to my parents. I did not understand why he was bringing that up now. For the first time I could not understand what he was getting at; his discussion appeared incoherent.

"Do you remember when we became engaged, Marianna, I promised to you and your parents that one day you could continue to study at university if you chose to."

"Yes, I do, but it wasn't a question of choice since before anything else I wanted to be married to you and have a family. I realized that to have both was impossible." I had no idea why we were talking about this now especially when we should be celebrating our daughter, I thought.

"Nothing is impossible," continued Michael with a smile.

"I know, but I also know that you can't have everything. I am happy with my life, though. I would not change it for anything."

"You don't have to change what you have, but you can add what you always wanted. I know that you enjoy learning; you do that every spare moment you have. I've heard that the University of Western Australia takes mature students, so there is nothing stopping you from attending."

"Why are we talking about this? The university might not accept me." I was starting to believe that all of this might be possible.

"I cannot see why not, especially when you have the qualifications that you have acquired over the years." Michael seemed knowledgeable about university entrance. Suddenly I realized that he knew something I didn't.

"Do you think I should apply, then?" I saw my daughter and my husband looking at one another with a smile. Something was certainly going on, something that I wasn't aware of.

"No, you don't have to apply," replied Michael.

"What then?"

"You don't have to apply because Natalie and I have already done so. There were two letters in the mail today. One was from the university for Natalie's acceptance and the other was for you. You have been accepted. Now it is all up to you. You can choose to fulfill your lifelong dream or refuse it."

I felt so lucky. These beautiful people, my wonderful family, had done this for me? I could not believe it. I went to throw my arms around their necks to give them a huge hug. I was so grateful for their amazing perception and sensitivity. I owed them so much. Suddenly I felt scared of failure, of letting them down. I had heard that university was like a different world. Would I be able to fit into a strange world? I was trembling with fear, a terrifying fear of the unknown. Michael, as usual, was sensing my mixed feelings of elation and trepidation.

"I am certain that you will conquer whatever frightens you. After a few weeks of university life, you will feel like you belong."

"Will I?" I asked.

"I have no doubt about it. Think about it. You came to Australia, an unknown world, and you have achieved more than anyone I know. You would not accept any negative treatment from anybody. You said once you could learn English and converse with people in their language, they would realize that people are fundamentally the same. They love and hurt in the same way and the cultural differences are minimal. It was just another way of seeing things.

"Those things, such as different customs and traditions, if shared, would enrich one another. And so it was. Because we have shared and have learned from a multicultural society, we are so much richer."

Michael looked at me, and smiling, he continued. "You knew this even before any antidiscrimination law was put in place. You knew that if you talked with them, cried with them, laughed with them, and love them, you could conquer the respect of the people of a nation."

"I think there's a little exaggeration there, to say the least. All the people of the nation do not even know I exist. I certainly didn't change their opinion."

"Perhaps not. But what I am trying to say is that if you set your mind to do something, you will succeed." I hugged my family once again and pondered whether I had the strength to attend university and whether or not I really wanted it at this stage of my life.

Of course, I wanted it. The question was could I do it? What if I failed? I hated failing. Regardless of this lack of confidence and the fear of failure, I had to try. I could not reject this astonishing gift that my husband and my family had given me. It was a gift from the heart, a promise made years ago and never forgotten. I somehow had to make sure that my husband's commitment to his word would be repaid by my dedication. I had to make sure that the passion I had for as long as I could remember, and thought would never come to fruition, would indeed be realized.

30

LIFE OF A STUDENT

"What was your life as a student like?" asked Leah.

"Yes, tell us all about it!" urged Jane. "Were you nervous? Were you treated well?"

"Yes, I was nervous. I'll never forget the first day. First of all, the campus was enormous, so I felt lost in a totally new world. I was trembling, and I think my knees were knocking together. Very soon though, when I realized how much learning I could do, I became immersed in my studies. There weren't many mature students then, but the young people were very kind."

"They did not treat you in the usual prejudicial way, or was the antidiscrimination act in place by then?"

The antidiscrimination law came later, but I did not notice any racial vilification at the university. People were there to learn the sciences and the arts, such as the history, the philosophy, and the literature of famous writers and poets of different countries of the world. Everyone had a dream to become the best he or she could be. There were the aspiring doctors, lawyers, engineers, and scientists.

The university was a place where everyone tried to develop him or herself and at the same time make a contribution to the world.

Without knowing it, equal opportunity was already in place at university. Everyone shared their experiences and knowledge, and friendship was not limited between age and race. If anything, those things were appreciated, because the citizenship did not belong to a country, but to the world. For me, every time I entered the campus, I felt like I was walking in a world where everything was possible. Was it just a dream? Perhaps. But it was better to dream of wonderful possibilities rather than live in world of negative realities.

"You did well at university, Nonna. Weren't you awarded a scholarship?"

"Yes, amazing, isn't it? Especially since I knew only two or three words of English when I came to Australia."

"It must have been difficult for you."

"Nothing worthwhile is ever easy. It wasn't just for me that I wanted to succeed, but I also aspired to leave an honorable legacy behind that my progeny would be proud of, and plus I did not want to let myself or my husband down, especially since he believed totally in me.

"As you know, our family in Sicily was well respected, but it meant nothing here. If we wanted respect in Australia, we had to start anew. We, had to earn it here. And that was exactly what I wanted to do. Thankfully my daughters, your aunt and your mother, were of the same opinion. As you know they are both well esteemed in their jobs and it appears that you, my granddaughters, are also wonderful achievers. I am so proud of all of you, and so is Nonno. We must never forget that it all started with him, with a promise that was never forgotten."

I could see that, as usual when I talked about the family and myself, both Leah and Jane would become a little emotional. I did not want them to think that my life had been only a struggle. Of course, there were times when the effort seemed unbearable, but we had to persist and continue on this, at times strenuous endeavor if we wanted to be truly part of a nation that at first had nothing but hostility toward us "aliens."

Regardless of the hard work that had to be done, I've had a good life. I have been happily married and had a wonderful family.

"Also, don't forget, Nonna, that you are what you always wanted to be, a university graduate," said Leah with a smile.

"Yes, Leah, I am very grateful for that. I have always thought that each one of us possesses a talent of some sort. It would be a shame if that talent, whether it seems extraordinary or ordinary, remained undeveloped."

"You said something else was important in life," said Jane pensively.

"Yes, I am sure. I've said so many things. Was it something in particular?"

"You said that it is important for a person to be able to make choices for his or her life."

"Oh, yes, I remember."

"Were you able to choose everything in your life?"

"I did not mean that you could choose every little thing in life. Of course, you can't. Some things are beyond our control. I remember saying that I did not have a choice for migrating to Australia. It was my father's decision, and we had to do what he determined was best for the family. So, for that, I had no control. I was too young anyway."

"You could have chosen later, as an adult."

"Yes, I could, and deep down I think I have."

31

THE MOTHERLAND

"Nonna, do you still think of Sicily?" Leah's question made me jump.

"Of course, I still think of Sicily. How can I not? Sicily is the land of my ancestors. It is the island where I was born and where my character was formed. As I witnessed what was good and what was bad, what was decent and what could be made better, it gave me a sense of purpose in life.

"As I was growing up in Sicily, I witnessed the maneuvers and the subterfuges of certain people. They used to hide and bury secrets for centuries to keep a kind of misguided sense of honor. I remember thinking that a hidden truth to preserve honor was far from honorable. As a young girl, I decided that it was much better to be open and honest regardless of the consequences. I remember that my dear friend Sara, in Sicily, used to say that "if one tells lies, one has to have a good memory." Since it is unlikely that one has a perfect memory right throughout life, it is easier to remember the truth rather than a fabricated lie. On a more positive side, I learned a deep sense of respect for people who had been my teachers, my mentors, and my friends. Their deep affection and their selfless and almost life-giving protection, gave me a sense of security and comfort."

"Nonna, you did not have a good time last time you went to Sicily, did you?" asked Jane

"No, I didn't."

"Why?"

"Because I was looking for things that the passing of time had changed. The second time I went I was at university. So, I did not have much time to visit the island. I went to visit a few universities to do some research for my postgraduate course. Ironic, isn't it?"

"Did you see anybody you knew? Did your relatives and friends remember you? Did they welcome you?" Leah wanted to know.

"Yes, there were people and relatives that still remembered me, and they would never forget the family name. And there is no question that I was welcomed. Sicilians know how to do that very well. What I admire about the Sicilian people is hospitality and their knowledge. Some of them might not have had an education, but they have the wisdom of the ages. The moon, the stars, and the sun guided their actions, and it was as if a person was one with nature and the whole universe."

"Was it sad for you … I mean, was it sad for you to leave once again?" Jane looked sad herself.

"Yes, it was sad because my sense of belonging was gradually disappearing. I felt a stranger in my own land. I felt that I had lost my place. People had the civility toward me that one has toward a stranger. I left Sicily with a sense of total devastation. I could never go back home because there was no home. I could go back to Sicily as a tourist, as a visitor, but not as a loving child to be embraced by the motherland."

"So, you made up your mind that you cannot stay in Sicily?"

"Oh, I can stay in Sicily. I can go and live there. I can gradually make a new home. But it would not be the continuation of the life that I used to have and know. I would have to start a new life again, almost like when I came to Australia."

"It would not be quite like when you came to Australia. At least you know the language," said Leah wisely.

"You are right; when I came to Australia, I did not know a word of English, but I can speak both Sicilian and Italian, plus I understand similar European languages. So yes, it would not be the same." I felt relieved.

"I realize more and more how difficult it must be to go and live in a country that you know little or nothing about and leave behind everything you had ever known. It must be such a sense of loss being away from the people and the place that you knew."

"Yes, Leah, it was! So much so that it is difficult for me to remember those times. When I do allow my memory to flood my being, I realize that my life has been an upward climb. However, on the other hand, the upward climb had been made easier with the love and support of my family, for without love and support, the ascending would have been impossible. The foot would have slipped back and there would have been a fall into the deepest abyss."

The girls looked at me, speechless. It was a good time to change the subject.

I smiled and said, "Nonno and I were thinking of going to Sicily with the whole family."

"How wonderful, Nonna. I would like to go to Sicily," said Leah assertively. Come to think of it, Leah was always assertive.

"So would I," repeated Jane.

"This time, together with all of you, it will be such a joy to show you my island. I will not think of what could have been, and I shall look at what is. We shall admire Sicily for its beauty, for its amazing different cultures and races of people molded into one, where every one of those ancient civilizations has left an indelible mark in the presence of castles, mosques, and breathtaking temples dedicated to the Greek gods."

"Oh, how wonderful!" shouted the girls.

"Hold on a second. We will have to ask your parents before I totally commit myself to the idea."

"Surely, they would not refuse. They would not dare."

"Let's wait until we ask them, shall we?"

The girls were right. The parents did not refuse, they would not dare. So, we started to prepare for a trip to Italy.

32

TRIP TO ITALY

Once we had decided to take the trip, we could not wait to go. There were six of us: my daughter Natalie and her husband, Raymond; their children, Leah and Jane; and of course my husband, Michael, and me. Our other daughter, Marie Teresa, and her husband, seasoned travelers, stayed behind.

We frantically organized the tour and packed our suitcases. We decided that before we went to Sicily, we should also visit some parts of the mainland. We started in the north, the Apennines to be exact. We rented a house high up on the mountain overlooking the lake of Garda. It was breathtaking scenery. We traveled around the nearby towns, and I felt that the place vaguely reminded me of something that my father had said when I was a young girl.

What was it? I put my hand on my forehead as if trying to extrapolate a memory from my brain. Oh, yes. I remembered now. A member of my family made history in this place. Turning to the family, I said: "My grandfather died in these mountains during the First World War."

"Which grandfather?" they asked.

"My father's father." I looked around and felt a chill in my body.

"I think we'd better go," I said. "This place makes me rather sad." They all agreed we should leave. In the days that followed we visited the city of Venice, which was an amazing experience, not for just for the girls but for all of us.

"How could they build a city on water?" asked Jane.

"It might seem as if it's built on water, but in actual fact, the city is built on more than a hundred small islands."

And down we went through towns and famous cities: Florence, Rome. "The city of Rome is called the Eternal City," said Leah.

"Why?" asked Jane?

This time it was her mother who answered. "It was the ancient Romans who thought that the Roman Empire would last forever and hence the word 'eternal.' I believe the dictum is still used in some documents. Perhaps, some Roman buildings appear to be lasting eternally since they were built. For instance, the Pantheon was commissioned by Marcus Agrippa and built in 120 AD, and the Colosseum was built around 70–80 AD. It is the iconic symbol of imperial Rome. It was originally called the Flavian Amphitheater and was capable of seating fifty thousand people. As you can see, these buildings are still standing."

"It's all so amazing, isn't it?" We all agreed.

"Our next stop is my hometown," said Michael. I could see that he was anxious to arrive at his town. He still had two sisters and a brother living there, plus nieces and nephews.

The welcome of Michael's town was unbelievable. Family, relatives, close friends, and possibly the not-so-close friends, were all waiting to greet us. There were embraces, questions, and laughter. And if the girls thought that Italians were loud in Australia, they had to rethink their outlook. In Australia, the Italian people restrained their emotions somewhat, for fear of being mocked, but here in their own country they were able to be themselves. And were they loud!

Maybe I should have warned the girls just in case they were traumatized, I thought to myself with a smile. Amusingly though, the girls were just as loud as the rest. It was remarkable to see that, even though their father was Australian, and their Italian was not so great, they could be understood.

Was this something genetic? I realized that they had comprehended that their hands could speak the language; actually, they could speak any language. It suddenly dawned on me that what they were saying about Italians was true. It goes something like this: "If you tie the hands of the Italians, they cannot speak at all." I must admit that my granddaughters had shown me that there was some truth in the saying.

My husband and I watched and were fascinated by what we saw. For the time that we were at my husband's town, the girls appeared to feel quite comfortable. They walked and talked with their cousins, with hands always flying up in the air, of course. They most definitely had learned the Italian language.

Soon we were in the car on the way to Sicily. I could not wait to see my Island again. The rest of the family appeared to be just as anxious as I was to arrive at our destination. From the autostrada, built on bridges that seemed to be attached to mountain peaks, the scenery was astounding; it took one's breath away. Since it was getting dark, we decided to spend the night at a hotel on the way.

In the morning, the sun was shining, and it appeared that it was going to be a magnificent day. We set out on our voyage toward the south. After a few hours of travel and many stops on the way, Leah, looking at the map said, "It should not be too long now."

"Oh! How exciting. Soon we will see Sicily," said Jane, clapping her hands.

"As soon as we reach the curve around the mountain, we should see the Tyrrhenian Sea and across the strait, the island of Sicily." My emotion was getting the better of me, and my voice was a little hoarse.

We went around the mountain and in the distance, we could see the island. We drove down to the Calabrian coast to the port of Villa San Giovanni where we could drive the car on the ferry that would take us across to Sicily. As soon as we parked the car on the boat, we went on deck to see the magnificent panorama. As we crossed the strait, Michael stood next to me and put his arm around me. As usual, my husband could read my mind.

"Many memories of your childhood," he said.

"Yes, a childhood spent too quickly, too hastily. When a child is given adult responsibilities at an early age, he or she loses that precious, carefree time."

"This happened to you, didn't it?"

"Yes, but it is too late for recriminations. Lost time cannot be recaptured." While Michael and I were talking, the girls came closer.

"The strait is very large, Nonna. I thought it would be narrower," stated Jane.

"Yes, it appears quite large. I think it takes about half an hour with a fast boat to cross it. There are so many legends about this place," I said, remembering the tales recounted to me long ago.

"What legends?" inquired Leah?

"A particular one comes to mind. It appears that Hercules swam across the strait with his herd of sacred cows. The monster Cariddi who lurked in these waters ate a few of the cows."

"That would have angered Hercules," said Leah with a smile.

"No doubt!"

While we were enjoying a few of the mythical stories that had survived through the ages, the boat was getting close to the island and the panorama was becoming clear. Suddenly our attention was focused on the phenomenon that was unfolding in front of our very eyes.

"Look, girls!" I said. "Look up on the mountain slope, behind that big building. Can you see that villa? That's where I was born. That villa belonged to us once. The name of the mountain is "Monte Santo," Holy Mountain in English. And look—look! That's the church where I was baptized, the Church of Christ the King."

"It's all so beautiful, Nonna. So, you were born on a holy mountain. Does that make you holy, Nonna?"

"No, I don't think so." We all smiled.

Looking around, I remembered another time, when as a migrant I was torn from my island and taken far away to another place in another world where for a time I felt feeble and weak. I remembered all the other people, full of hope, shouting promises from the ship Australia to their loved ones—promises they probably could not keep. And here I was, almost a lifetime later, or at least it seemed a lifetime. Or was it only yesterday? Time has a way of going by without warning, without consideration. Tomorrow appears in the now without notice. Our life seems a swift run to desperately try to catch up with our plans and dreams.

"I feel that I have traveled full circle," I said to Michael.

I'm back from where I came. It feels as if the young girl never left, and the older woman with her beautiful family is back. Perhaps she is back to pick up that young girl whom she left behind. "How cruel!" I said, not realizing that I had spoken aloud.

"What's cruel?" asked Michael.

"Nothing. I was just thinking out aloud." Fortunately, the girls interrupted my erratic thoughts.

"Nonna, look at that tall statue? What is it?"

"It is a statue of Our Lady of the Letter."

"I never heard that before. What does it mean, 'Our Lady of the Letter?'"

"I was actually born on her feast day, so I heard quite a bit about it from my mother and grandmother. The story goes that when Saint Paul came to Sicily, the people of Messina welcomed him, and they believed in his preaching of Jesus. It is said that Mary, the mother of Christ, wrote a letter to the people of Messina blessing them for their faith."

"There's something written at the base of the statue. Is that Latin?" asked Jane.

"Yes, it is. It says, Vos ET Ipsam Civitatem Benedicimus, which means, "We bless you and your city."

These were the last words I had read before leaving the port of Messina on my way to Australia, and they had stuck in my mind, but I said nothing to my family—I did not want to spoil the moment. Our crossing of the strait was over. We got into the car to go to our destination. It took us about an hour and a half by car to arrive there. The house where we were staying was not too distant from the place where I had gone to school. Looking down the beautiful valley, we could see the place where we used to live. There were acres and acres of fertile land, "as far as the eyes could see," Nonna would have said, that had belonged to the Del Feo family. I did not want to go there just yet; I wasn't ready.

The following day we started our tour around the island. To the tourist, it is a place like no other. Its scenery is wonderful, and it is a place where thousands of years of history can be learned, simply by looking at its churches, palaces, museums, and theaters. Our first stop was Cefalù. The coffee and sweets were delicious.

"Are there any stories about Cefalù, Nonna?" asked Leah.

"There are stories about every town of Sicily. Or should I say there is history, which is elaborated with great stories. For instance, look at the magnificent cathedral," I said, pointing across the piazza where we were having our coffee. "The cathedral was commissioned by Roger II, Norman King of Sicily. It is said that the sand was brought from Jerusalem. Apparently, he had made a vow to the Holy Savior that he would bring the sand from Jerusalem if he were granted the grace he asked for; obviously he must have received the miracle."

"It is beautiful!" They uttered. I could see that my family was impressed.

"Perhaps we should purchase a book which will explain the things you will be seeing," I said, but Jane objected.

"I saw some of the books and they are not much fun. They haven't all the nice stories, only history." We looked at one another and realized that, according to Jane, being told about the place was, perhaps, much better than reading about it.

"Our next stop will be Palermo, the capital of Sicily. There we will see another example of magnificent architecture called the Palatina Chapel, also commissioned by Roger II in 1132."

When we arrived at Palermo, we went into the Palatina Chapel, which is situated in the Royal Palace. The architecture is Norman-Arabic, and the mosaics are of Byzantine origin. "What amazing work!" They all agreed.

What a stupendous city. Palermo's Theater (Teatro Massimo) is one of the biggest in Europe. There are eight magnificent churches in the historical center of Palermo.

"How many churches are there in Palermo, Nonna?" asked Leah.

"About 152, I think."

"We not going to visit all of them, are we?"

"No, Jane. We could not possibly see all of them. To see all the churches, not counting all the other beautiful places, we would have to stay at least a year in Palermo. Maybe another time."

I heard Natalie ask the girls, "It's a beautiful place, isn't it? Did you ever imagine that Sicily would be so beautiful?"

"Nonna had told us that it was a beautiful Island, but one has to see it to believe it. We thought that Nonna could have been a bit biased seeing that she was born here." They all laughed.

I was so happy that they enjoyed themselves; they appeared to be at home.

"I am glad you all think that I wasn't biased."

33

THE ROYAL MOUNTAIN
(MONREALE)

Monreale, from the Latin Mons Regalis (literally meaning "Royal Mountain") is situated on the slopes of Mount Caputo.

"Is this place very high, Nonna?"

"No, not that high. About three hundred meters above sea level."

"And that's not high? Compared to Western Australia it is very high."

"Not as high as some of the places we have been and some of the other places we have yet to go. As for Western Australia, it is rather flat in comparison to Sicily."

As soon as we arrived in Monreale, the first stop as usual was for us to run to the pasticceria and have our coffee with the wonderful, sweet treats the place had to offer, which differed from city to city. Sicily was renowned for its delicious cakes. After having done that, we went sightseeing. The town of Monreale overlooks the Conca d'Oro, as the valley beyond Palermo is called. It seems that, as I recall, this place has two different names in English: "Basin of Gold" and the "Golden Shell."

"Why is it called Conca d'Oro?"

"As you can see down there," I said, pointing down the valley, "there is a citrus grove. When the sun is shining on the citrus fruit it gives a kind of golden glow, hence Conca d'Oro. Of course, it used to be much larger before but a lot of it, unfortunately, has been sacrificed to progress." My family was staring in wonder at the panorama, where judging from the ancient buildings, different races of people had come together to demonstrate their skills and artistry.

William II called, "the good," commissioned the cathedral and the Abbey of Monreale. It is said William was very devout to Mary. One day when he went hunting and after walking for a long period of time, he became very tired. He lay down under a carob tree and fell asleep. In his sleep, Mary appeared to him and said, "William, in the same spot where you are sleeping, there's a great treasure hidden. Dig it out and build a church in the same place." As soon as the Madonna said that she disappeared. When King William awoke, he called his men to dig under the tree. They dug, and, in fact, found all the gold that was needed for the building of the Duomo.

It appears that William wanted to outdo his father, William I, "the bad." He obviously did just that, because the Duomo exceeds the beauty of any church we have ever seen. The cathedral and the abbey represent the culmination of the most magnificent Norman art.

Many cultures had come together including the Norman, the Arab, and the Byzantine, to make it the best artistic expression the world has ever seen. Am I exaggerating? Perhaps, but I have never seen anything like this, and judging by the other tourists in the cathedral, they felt the same way. My family looked astonished.

"This is amazing. It is so grand. One may say that the East and the West have come together to create all of this," whispered Leah.

"That's exactly right."

"There is so much gold, and that Jesus is so big," said Jane, pointing at the "big Jesus."

"You mean the Christ Pantocrator. The word pantocrator is a Greek word, which means 'ruler of all.' As you can see, he has the book of the sacred word in his left hand and his right hand is raised in blessing. If you look closely at his right hand, his fingers are shaped in the letters of IC. XC. The letters signify the Greek words of Issues Khristos."

I was feeling a little tired of the voluntary job I had taken up, that of a cicerone. So, I looked in silence at this awesome and magnificent building; there were no words to give justice to this place, anyway. There is a saying that no visit to Palermo is complete without seeing Monreale. This has to be true.

As we descended to Palermo, we silently said goodbye to this creation of a time when differences had been put aside in order to offer the best that one could possibly offer. History was witness to this amazing human effort.

34

A Soundless Sicily

The streets of Sicily are full of noises: noises of cars, of people, of children, and other noises. One might say that, as far as noises go, it's no different from any other part of the world. Sicily, however, has another side, which is probably unknown or invisible to the tourist. Is it the Mafia? No! I am told that the Mafia has gone out of fashion. It seems that the new generation has said "No" in a fairly loud voice to the Mafia's influence on the people. When people lose the fear of something, that thing is rendered useless. Or so I am told. However, I must admit that the Mafia acted in extreme silence. Apparently, the discussions that the Mafia bosses had with their dependents were silent—no words, just signs.

However, since it is not the Mafia that I want to discuss, I shall try to recount some of the tales of "silent Sicily." There is a town in Sicily, actually the one we are heading to, that has fascinated me since I had read about it as a child. This town is famous because

Virgil mentioned it in Aeneid. To visit this town, one has to go up and then up some more.

"Nonna, this place is frightening." This time all my family agreed with Jane's comment. What was more frightening to me was the fact that Raymond was driving. It worried me immensely because he was used to drive on the Western Australian plains rather than the Italian peaks. Looking at him, though, if he was nervous, he did not show it. In fact, he looked very calm and collected. I had no idea how he could do that.

"Will we ever get there?" I was having my own doubts of ever getting there especially since I was suffering from acrophobia myself. I wondered why on earth I had convinced my family to reach for the sky. I guess all my life I had tried to reach for the sky, and now I was going to touch it.

As we went up, the clouds were on top of us, on the side of us, and everywhere. I prayed as I had never prayed before. The one consolation about this predicament was that we could not see the big drop on the side of the mountain or else we would all be petrified, not that we were not terrified now.

"Are we ever going to reach this town?"

"We had better reach it, especially since we cannot turn the car around." As soon as I said that I realized that it was the last thing I should have said. Not only had I terrorized my family, but myself also.

As we turned the corner a bus was coming toward us. I thought to myself that there were two things that could happen to us: the bus could hit us and we would die, or send us down on the side of the mountain, and we would die. But thank God, there was a third option that I had not considered. The bus almost scraped past us without really touching our car and the driver went down the mountain without realizing the turmoil that he had caused in us. The sigh of relief from everyone was heard in the car.

"This place had better be worth it," my family complained. I felt the same.

"I am sure it is. So many stories and legends have been written about this place."

"What is the name of this town? Asked Jane.

"Erice." I replied.

Finally we had arrived. Erice in its majesty was standing in front of us, not that we could see much since the fog was so amazingly thick. We parked our car and carried our suitcases up the slope toward the hotel where we were supposed to stay.

"We are still climbing." My family was exhausted.

"Yes, but as I understand our hotel is not too far."

For a moment I wished I were back on the flat terrain of Western Australia.

The hotel where we would be staying was indeed not too far. It appeared suddenly in front of us. There were sighs of relief and grateful thanks to God for our safe arrival.

The fog, like a blanket, had covered the town completely. It was as if the sky had descended upon us and there was no escape.

"It is quite eerie," I said.

"You can say that again."

"Do we have to stay here?" asked Jane.

"You don't want to go down the mountain in this darkness, do you?" Leah was determined to see this adventure through. She was the most adventurous among all of us.

We went to our hotel to check in and have our suitcases delivered to our rooms. Even the town appeared totally uninhabited; we decided to look around the place to try to find some sort of life. Surely there would have to be people living here. It was a town, after all.

Michael looked and me and smiled. "It is a heavenly place."

"Do you think?"

"Yes. The night is dark and eerie and it has the right atmosphere."

The girls came closer and wondered whether there weren't any shops in this "weird place."

"I am sure there are. I am told it is a famous tourist place."

"Are you joking? What would tourists do in a place where the fog is so thick that one cannot see a meter in front of them?"

"The fog does not descend on the town all the time."

"I thought because the town is near the sky, the clouds would be here all the time," said Jane, convinced that we were in the clouds.

"This place is high, but I don't really think it reaches the sky."

"Do you know that according to legend, the nymphs are lurking around the place, especially on a noiseless night like this? If you look closely, my grandmother used say, you can see them."

"What do they look like? Are they like angels?"

"I don't know what they look like; I have never seen one. All I know is what I have been told and what I have read in books. The artist represents them as being very pretty and playful. It seems that nymphs can be quite mischievous, while the angels are completely good."

"Why are they mischievous? What do they do?"

"When no one is watching, they can steal something that belongs to you and never return it." The girls clutched at their purses, and Michael and the others burst out laughing.

"There is another story where the nymphs are good. According to the ancient Greek historian, Diodoro Siculo, it seems that Hercules, swimming with his sacred cows, arrived here. The nymphs, realizing that after his enormous voyage he would be exhausted, opened up baths with hot water to alleviate his tiredness. It seems that these baths still exist in the towns of Imera and Segesta."

"So, Hercules traveled from east to west of Sicily, all in one go?" Leah was smiling.

"Actually, when he swam across the Strait of Messina, he had already traveled a long distance, and when he arrived in Sicily, he swam around the Island, not just across it."

"Thank God for his sacred cows." Someone giggled.

"It wasn't just the cows. It appears that he was a very strong boy who had performed many heroic feats. Hercules was the son of Zeus and Alcmene. Hera, Zeus's wife, was jealous of the baby Hercules so she sent him some snakes. The snakes were placed in his cradle but, with his strength, he had no problem strangling the snakes.

"It seems that one of his heroic deeds was accomplished when he arrived here in Erice. Apparently, he had a battle with the king. The pact was that if the King Erix, the son of Aphrodite and Bute, won, Hercules would give him his sacred bulls, and if Hercules won, the King would give him his kingdom. Of course, the hero won, and he conquered the kingdom and killed the king."

"Did Hercules stay here then?"

"No, he went away."

"With his sacred cows?"

"No, he left them here on his own land."

"There must be a lot of sacred bulls in Sicily!"

"No doubt." Now everyone was laughing. The noise that we made was the only sound around the town.

"What happened next?"

"The Greeks came in and conquered the land and, one would assume, also the sacred bulls."

"So are you saying that when we eat meat it could be sacred?"

"Oh, I had never thought of it like that, but it could be a possibility. That would explain why the food is so delicious."

As we walked and talked, we arrived at the center of the town, where lights were piercing through the fog. What a relief! Finally we could see each other. As usual we entered the pasticceria to have our cappuccino with cake. Later we would have dinner at our hotel. We could only see our surroundings as far as the small piazza. We asked whether this fog was a constant in Erice. They replied that even though it did come down in the late afternoon, on this particular day, it had been worse than they could remember. Then they asked us whether we were stranieri (foreigners). We told them we came from Australia without mentioning that Sicily was my birthplace. Michael looked at me, and I shrugged my shoulders.

We retired to our hotel, and our dinner was delicious. When we went to our rooms, we hoped that tomorrow would be a better day and we would be able to see what made this town famous. Before going to bed, Michael and I looked out the window, but there was nothing to be seen. On dark nights like these, the people retired indoors early. The houses built in the narrow streets were protected and hermetically closed by thick doors and door shatters. Once inside, the people cooked the evening meal; but the wonderful odors escaped and filled the town, regardless of their tight enclosure.

After dinner, softly, as I remembered, stories were told. I never knew why the voices were lowered especially when the mythological tales were recounted. Perhaps it was to give the story a sense of foreboding and thus capture the attention of the children, whom in turn would have to relate it to their children and pass them down the ages.

Was this oral history? It was something or other! I don't think people who told the story in the silence of the night knew themselves. They were the stories of ancient civilizations that had been passed on to this day. One thing was certain. Children would stay indoors rather than be confronted by the mischievous nymphs who flew and giggled in the night. The darker the night, the better—they all assembled and plotted together.

"Are you OK?" asked Michael, the love of my life.

"Yes. Why?"

"You looked very pensive."

"Oh, it's nothing! I was just thinking of the events of the day. There is a story that I omitted telling the girls. I didn't feel comfortable relating it to them."

"What story is that?"

"The story of the so-called sacred prostitution, which in ancient times was practiced here in Erice. I guess this was part of the cult in honor of the goddess of love Aphrodite, or Venus as the Romans called her."

"Sacred prostitution? I knew that in ancient times this was practiced in the East and Middle East, by the Babylonians, the Phoenicians, Assyrians, and others, but I didn't know that it was practiced here in Erice."

"It appears that it was brought here by those people. In those days the sacred prostitution was not considered degrading; it was a giving of oneself to the gods. I guess that's why it was called 'sacred.' It is believed that here in Erice it was performed in the temple dedicated to Aphrodite. Apparently, there were different kinds of sacred prostitution. In the so-called Hierodule, the priestesses, consecrated to the gods, were offered to those who visited the temple. In Hierogamy, sex was considered a revered, mystical, and spiritual act that symbolized the union between two deities."

"Very interesting. We will be visiting the temple tomorrow, won't we?" said Michael jokingly with his wonderful smile.

"Let me stress that it is not happening anymore!"

We both laughed, and changing the subject, I asked, "Do you think our grandchildren are enjoying themselves? It wasn't a good day to arrive here. It is so dark and almost frightening."

"I think that's why they liked the town. The story of Hercules and of course that of the nymphs was very appropriate for a day like today. Don't worry!" he said, embracing me. "Tomorrow, according to the maître d'hôtel, it is going to be a beautiful day."

We looked out the window and there was nothing at all to be seen or heard. Where were the inhabitants and where was the panorama, which, according to the people, was out of this world? Exaggeration? Perhaps. We would know for certain tomorrow. Now we were exhausted, and it was time for bed and a good night's sleep. After our incessant traveling, we needed a restful night. Tomorrow will come what may.

35

PARADISE ON EARTH

A knock on the door made me jump, and for a moment I wasn't aware where I was. I sat up and realized that I had overslept.

"I think our family is knocking at the door," said Michael.

"You must have been awake for a long time. You look ready to go out. Look at me, I am hardly awake, and I haven't even showered yet. Michael, why didn't you wake me up?"

"You were extremely tired, and you needed your sleep, Marianna."

I hugged him and said, "You always know what I need." I quickly put my dressing gown on and went to the door.

"Aren't you ready, Nonna?"

"No, but I will be in a few minutes."

"We can wait for you," said Natalie, but I could see that the girls were anxious to go out.

"No, you go. Papà is ready; he can come down to breakfast with you, and I will catch up with you as soon as I can."

"I'll wait for you." Michael was determined to escort me to breakfast. Turning to our family he said, "You go ahead, we will not be long."

I showered quickly and got ready in record time.

"I must admit, I feel much better after my good sleep."

"I know—you look beautiful."

I smiled at him, and hand in hand we walked toward the hotel restaurant.

"By the way, what is the weather like? I didn't even get the chance to look out of the window."

"The weather is beautiful, and the sun is shining. And it's just as well that you did not look outside the window."

I was about to ask him what he meant when he said that it was just as well that I had not looked out of the window, when the girls came to greet us.

"Have you started breakfast?"

"No, we were waiting for you."

I could see that everyone was in a hurry to go outdoors, but the food that was placed in front of us was scrumptious. The waiter went past our table with a trolley and on it there were croissants, brioches, and every delectable cake. The room was filled with the wonderful aroma of coffee. We ate as quickly as we could to escape outdoors where the golden sunshine was visible. It was a beautiful day after all. Who could have thought that from the darkness of the previous day it was even remotely possible that the sun brought so much light?

Finally, we were dashing outside into the street. The shops were opening up, but the place was still relatively quiet. Having noticed that everyone appeared relaxed, we also slowed our step and went with the unhurried stride of the rest of the people. "Up here near the sky," as the girls put it, there is no reason to run.

We looked around amazed with the orderliness of the place. The narrow streets were paved with concrete insets, in which the cobbled paving appears like a beautiful mosaic. The gray stone walls of the buildings in the narrow streets where the people had balconies were decorated with beautiful, bright flowers. We walked around in silence in order to respect the soundless atmosphere. I had read so much about this enchanting place that I was almost afraid of disappointing my family and myself. Deep down, though, by looking at the people and the way they gracefully walked and gently talked, one could see that they were representing a noble mannerism that they had inherited from their ancestors. They simply witnessed who they were.

Coming out of the narrow streets in the open space, a beautiful park was extending before us. Overwhelmed, I sat down on one of the benches. Unaware that I had stayed behind, Michael and the family were walking ahead.

When Michael realized that I had remained some distance away, he came right back and asked, "Are you tired, Marianna?"

"No, just overwhelmed by this sunshine and the beauty of this place. I want to take it all in gradually."

"I don't think we have seen anything yet. Come with me, let's go toward the castle. It looks amazing."

"Indeed, everything looks magnificent."

There are two castles in Erice. The Pepoli castle, which dates from the Saracen times, and the Venus castle, dating from the Norman period, built on top of the ancient temple of Venus, where Venus Ericina was worshipped. According to legend, Aeneas founded the temple.

Michael and I walked slowly toward what appeared to be the very edge of the mountain, and at the foot of it we could see the city of Trapani, a relatively modern city. Because Erice is situated at the very corner of the triangle that is Sicily, one can see a wonderful panorama both left and right at an enormous distance.

But what suddenly fascinated me were the islands that were visible from Erice. They were the Aegadian Islands, where myth and history mingle. There are three major islands: Favignana, Levanzo, and Marettino. As someone said, "To see the Aegadian Islands from Erice is priceless." It is indeed priceless; one can imagine the body of the dead Anchises, the father of Aeneas being brought here for his burial. Apparently, somewhere in this place there is a stele that is said to be Anchises's burial place.

In book five of The Aeneid we read Virgil's story of when Aeneas, because of a storm, was pushed away from the route toward Italy, which he had intended to take, and instead was pushed toward Erice. As his helmsman said to him, "I think that the friendly coastline of Erix your brother and Sicily's havens are not far off."

This was also the place where Elimo, Aeneas's half brother, lived. The Elyms or Elymian people, who lived in the western corner of the island, were named for him. According to the Greek historian Thucydides, the Trojan refugees (who were defeated by the Greeks) founded Erice.

As if in a trance, I jumped when Michael spoke to me. "I was looking at the map of the place this morning," he said, "and down at Trapani there are roads called Aeneas Passage and Via Virgil."

"I was thinking of Aeneas's supposed passage from the islands to Erice, and you are telling me that there is a place named after him? As always you seem to read my mind, Michael."

"Of course! I saw you looking at those magnificent islands and you had to be thinking of Aeneas's entrance into Erice."

"Apparently, he received a great welcome by the King Aceste, who was the son of a Trojan woman and a river god named Crimisus. He had witnessed the arrival of the ships. Realizing that the ships belonged to friends, he came to greet them. He was delighted to see people of his own background."

"What a fantastic story. The girls will want to hear it."

"I think they know parts of it. I briefly mentioned it before."

"Nonna, is this where Aeneas came before he found Rome?" Leah asked.

"As legend has it, this is the very place."

"How come he stopped here?" inquired Jane.

"It seemed that a hazardous storm brought the ships to this corner of the island. Aeneas was warned not to come toward Sicily. He was told that the giants Scylla and Charybdis engulfed everything in sight, not to mention the Harpies.

"Who were the Harpies?"

"Apparently, they looked like very ugly old women with wings. When I was a young girl and hearing these stories, I thought I saw the Harpies. It was a dark windy night and, knowing what they were capable of, I was very frightened."

"Why? What do they do, Nonna?"

"Do you want to really know this?"

"Yes, we do."

"On a stormy, windy night, that's when they usually come out. They used to snatch the people and take them to the underground where there is no return. So, Aeneas, even though he was destined to come because of his mission to found Rome, was frightened. Who could blame him? He could have been the prey of the Harpies or else could have been eaten alive by the monsters. Either way it was very unpleasant, to say the least.

"But good old Poseidon, the god of the sea, assured him that he would look after him and, I guess, that is why Aeneas was pushed this way. As fate would have it, his father, Anchises, was buried here and since it was one year after his death, they decided to have the games in his honor. According to Virgil, there is also the story of the snake."

"What story of the snake?" asked the girls with the impatience of youth.

"Let me take a breath, and I will tell you."

"Did the snake try to hurt Aeneas?"

"I can see that I am not permitted to breathe, so I will continue," I said with a smile.

"Aeneas, before talking to the spirit of his father, graced his head with his mother's myrtle and his people did the same. His mother was Venus. Then, as a tribute to his father, he poured on the earth two bowls of wine, two bowls of fresh milk, and two bowls of deified blood and scattered flowers around the place.

"He was talking to his dead father, telling him of his intended journey to reach the Tiber, but he had no idea where that might be. When he finished talking, a gigantic snake appeared. It was slithering toward the bowls. It tasted their contents and then ate the offerings placed on the altar and slithered back from whence it came. Everyone was amazed, and Aeneas wondered whether the snake, of magnificent golden colors, was some vigilant power of the place or his father's spirit. This is something we will never know."

I had finished talking and now I simply wanted to bask in the beauty of this place.

Michael, who had the eye of an architect, said, "This place is shaped in an equilateral triangle, and on some of its edges there are the most remarkable buildings. For instance, I read somewhere that La Chiesa Madre was initially a little sacred edifice built under the Empire of Constantine. For the foundation, some stones of the Temple of Venus were used, and ultimately the magnificent church was constructed in 1312 under the order of Aragonese King Frederic II. It seems that he lived in Erice for quite some time."

"I can see that you have done your own research about the place."

"Who can help it? It's a place like no other."

"When you said that Erice is shaped in an equilateral triangle, I suddenly realized that Sicily itself, is also a roughly triangular shape."

"Yes, of course. That's why it was called Trinacria," replied Michael.

Later, we went to the fountain of Venus. We saw that people were throwing money in the fountain of Venus like they do in the fountain of Trevi. I guess they thought that the coin they threw in the water would grant them their wish to return.

We heard a clock chime, which told us that it was lunchtime. Actually, judging from everyone's demeanor, we needed no clock to tell us that we were all famished. We all agreed that we should look for a restaurant to have lunch. It was not difficult to find, since one of the streets was full of shops, restaurants, and cafés. The smell of food, sweets, and coffee filled the air. We entered one of the restaurants, and a waiter greeted us and escorted us to a table.

We were told to taste pasta with a Trapanese pesto, which was different from the pesto I knew. The one I was used to was green and made with basil, but the Trapanese pesto was red and delicious. We ate our scrumptious lunch, and I bought a jar of pesto simply because I wanted to reproduce the recipe. It was Natalie who guessed my intention.

"You want to make this pesto, don't you, Mamma?"

"Yes, it should not be too difficult. There are the ingredients listed on the jar."

"I am sure you can do it."

"Of course, the jar does not list the quantity of the ingredients, but that will be a matter of taste and I definitely will never forget the wonderful taste."

"Nor I," replied Natalie.

We slowly went toward the hotel to have our afternoon siesta. We were getting accustomed to our siesta since everyone seemed to disappear from the face of the earth in the afternoon.

When we got up fully rested, I thought that a visit to the shops was in order.

"I told our family to go ahead and meet us later. I knew that you want go shopping, and you probably want to do this on your own." I don't know how Michael did it, but he knew my inner thoughts.

"Have you spoken to Raymond? Is he having a good time? Perhaps the fact that he doesn't understand much Italian makes him sort of lonely. I don't want him isolated."

"Haven't you noticed that nearly everyone understands English and that he converses to his wife and daughters and us? Don't worry, everyone is fine."

"Michael, are you coming shopping with me?"

"I think you would be better off on your own. I will go for a walk, and we can all meet in the piazza later."

"Do you know whether there is going to be much fog this afternoon?"

"I was told that there would not be as much as yesterday."

We all went our separate ways. I went to a shop that I had noticed this morning. It sold tapestries made locally. They were unique and beautiful with stunning colors and designs. It would be nice to buy a few for family and friends. I went into the shop and was greeted by a very gentle and soft-spoken lady. She asked me if I was interested in something in particular. I told her I had noticed the beautiful tapestries and asked if she could show me some. She brought different ones, and I fell in love with them. She told me that they were made on the loom locally. I told her that I knew because I had read it on the notice in the window.

"You speak Italian very well, Signora. You can read it also."

"Yes, I can read and speak Italian."

"You are not from these parts, are you?" And then embarrassed that she had been questioning me, added, "I am sorry for being a little inquisitive."

"Not at all. I was born in Sicily and went to school here, but then my family emigrated to Australia, and I have been living there most of my life."

"Australia? That's so far away."

"Yes, it is."

"Will you ever come back here to live?"

"At first, I thought I would, but then I realized that I am as much a stranger here as I was when I went to Australia. But who knows?" I said, shrugging my shoulders. It was so pleasant talking to this lady. I could see that she had that gift to make people feel truly welcome.

I finished choosing all the different things that I wanted to bring back with me and paid what she asked, shook her hand goodbye, and went out of the shop. I was going toward the place where I was supposed to meet my husband when I heard someone calling me, "Signora, Signora." At first, I thought that the person was calling someone else, but, as I turned around, I realized that it was the lady of the shop calling me and signaling me to stop.

"May I talk with you, please?"

"Yes, of course. Did I forget something?"

"No," she replied, "I did." I was puzzled, but as she came running to me, I noticed she had a parcel in her hand.

"When you paid for the things you bought, you did not ask for a discount, and I did not give you any."

Still puzzled, I said, "I was told that in your shop there was no discount, and one must pay the price marked on the items."

"Normally that's how it is. But because you are such a special lady, I want to give you a little gift." I was astounded. No one had ever done something like this before. I looked in the bag and saw a beautiful tapestry.

"Please accept this. It has the Christmas colors, and when you use it, think of us."

"I most certainly will. Thank you so much; you are so very kind." I could not help myself and gave the beautiful lady a hug.

"Maybe we should have a coffee together and talk about this wonderful place," she suggested. "We can go to the caffè next door. People usually know I go there to talk to my friend. Wait a moment while I place a notice in the window."

We sat down at a corner table, and I said, "Erice has fascinated my family and me. It is a place where legends still live on."

"It is difficult to wipe away the ideology of legends that have survived for thousands of years. Sicily will always have a story to tell."

"I am well aware of that. I still remember my grandmother telling us stories, and we listened so attentively in case we missed something of what she was saying."

"It made our childhood rich and life in general interesting. Mythology, for instance: Homer's Iliad and Odyssey written around 750 BC and 650 BC are still taught in schools and universities. Not to mention Virgil's Aeneid, which is considered "the gateway of the pagan and the Christian centuries." Virgil, who was born in 70 BC and died in 19 BC speaks of Aeneas passing through our town before going to Rome. No one can say for certain that there isn't some truth in all these stories."

The lady, as she spoke almost with conviction, left me spellbound, like when I was a child listening to my nonna; for a while I felt that time had stood still.

"Like us, our children have always been told the tales of the ancient world, and I am certain they will relate the stories to their children and to their children's children. The stories will not influence them in any negative way. On the contrary, wherever life takes them, they will have wonderful memories of their youth."

It definitely felt that this wise lady was talking about me, and I replied, "You are right. No matter where you go, far away or near, you will never forget your birthplace."

"You would know it, wouldn't you?"

"Yes." I sighed.

"Will you come and see us again?"

"I would like to."

"I have a feeling that in the not-too-distant future we will see one another again. I feel that we will meet again or else we would not have made a friendship almost instantaneously like we did." I agreed, but then again who was I to disagree with Sicilian prophecy? We reluctantly said our goodbyes and departed from one another.

Later, when I met Michael and the family and told them what the lady had done and said, they were amazed.

"So, you made a friend?"

"Yes."

We walked in a leisurely fashion around the main street when a waiter offering canapés and liqueurs greeted us. He told us that that the offering was with the compliments of the shop where all the delicacies were sold and pointed us toward the building. I tasted liqueur made with prickly pears. It was delicious.

The evening was magical; the fog had not descended on the town like the previous night. We were able to look at the town and the people. We could stroll and look in the windows of the shops. Looking at the walls, we were able to read the different stages of occupation by the Elymian people and the Phoenicians. We could feel the destruction caused by the Punic war between Carthage and Rome. One only had to look at each stone of the place to interpret its history. It was a place of relaxation, recreation, and learning.

"I will never forget this place." I thought. Looking at my family, I saw that they felt the same way.

"Was it worth it climbing to the sky, Jane?"

"Oh, yes," she replied.

"Maybe we should ask your dad. He literally did the climbing."

"Was it worth it, Dad?"

"Yes, I would most definitely do it again."

"Next time we will take the cable car."

Changing the subject, I said, "We are leaving this place tomorrow."

There was a chorus of "Nooooooooooo!"

36

THE DORIC TEMPLES

We reluctantly left the triangle in the clouds where people walk with pride and talk with humility. They attend church every Sunday and still relate the pagan legends of the ancient world. They believe in their guardian angel and still consider that the mischievous nymphs might float around on a dark foggy night to cause a problem or two, in the form of a broken vase of flowers that has fallen on the pavement from the balustrade of a balcony or a shattered glass from a window.

And now we were descending into what we might call the normal world: where people walk fast, talk louder, and perhaps are a little arrogant. It is as if we have flicked the page of the book of life where everything is neither past nor future. It is as the past does not belong to us and the unknown future brings fear, if anything. So, we run away from yesterday and try to avoid tomorrow.

How blissful was the silent and quiet Erice, where people know where they come from because they realize that the past, whether we like or not, impacts the present, and the good actions of the present give them the promise of a serene future. I was already missing Erice.

Going down the mountain wasn't nearly as terrifying as going up. Perhaps because we knew where we were going, we did not have the dreaded fear of the unknown. Nevertheless, we did breathe a sigh of relief when we reached flat ground. Not that the flat ground was the norm in Sicily, on the contrary. I was sure that we still had to do a considerable amount of climbing to see the rest of the Island. However, we were almost becoming experts in "reaching for the stars."

As the historians would say: "The history of Sicily begins with the Greek colonization which began toward the middle of the eighth century BC." The history of the Greeks in Sicily is undeniable because it is ingrained in stone. The Doric temple built on Elymian soil on the beautiful green hill of Segesta some seventy-five kilometers from Palermo not only testifies to the Greek historical presence in Sicily, but also the gargantuan legacy left for future generations on the island. The Temple of Segesta is something that leaves the onlookers perplexed. It is a most magnificent construction: it was built some 2,400 years ago, and yet it appears as if it was finished only recently.

There is confusion among scholars as to whom the temple was dedicated to; some attribute the dedication of the temple to Ceres, the mother of Persephone; others to Diana and still others to Venus. According to Cicero (In Verrem, IV), there existed a temple of Diana in Segesta. However, one thing is certain. The temple in Segesta left all of us speechless, something that rarely happens, if at all. When someone finally spoke, I heard Leah and Jane say, "There is no need to go to Greece to see Greece because one can see Greece in Sicily." I had never thought it that way before, but their assertion indeed had merit.

After going into the temple and around it, we had to have our coffee and of course in Sicily where there is something, anything, there is a caffè. We had our usual coffee with a piece of delicious torta without much conversation. We all seemed to realize that while everything around us changes, beauty remained ageless, and we were all in awe of it.

We went down the west coast of Sicily and around it. Every spot we visited had either a story to tell or history to teach. For instance, Selinunte, visible by the destruction of its temples, was evidence of the ancient devastation inflicted by the Carthaginians, while Calatafimi and Marsala told a more recent historical event— the entrance of Garibaldi for the unification of Italy.

We arrived at Agrigento (called Akragas by the Greeks), one of the cities of the Magna Graecia. Apparently, the Carthaginians had sacked the city, and it is said that it did not recover completely to its earlier prominence. The Romans restored it somewhat later.

Yet the Valley of the Temples remains one of the most important archaeological sites of Sicily and the most awesome. Looking at the beautiful temples one wonders how from 510–430 BC, a time when humanity lacked the building resources it has today, they could have been erected. I guess every era has the talents to accomplish things that appear almost impossible and incomprehensible to others.

"There are seven temples, Nonna," shouted Jane from a distance.

"Yes, there are. Did you read the names of the gods they were dedicated to?"

"Yes, we made a list." Leah was always logical and systematic.

"Read it to us!"

"Juno, Concord, Asclepius, Heracles, Zeus, Dioscuri, Vulcan."

"Juno's Greek name is Hera. According to Greek mythology, she was the goddess of marriage."

"What about Asclepius?"

"He was the son of Apollo and was the god of medicine and healing."

"I know who Heracles was!" asserted Jane excitedly. "He is Hercules, the one who was swimming with his sacred cows."

"Exactly! He was also a hero because he was very strong."

"As for Zeus—he was the god of lighting and thunder."

"What about Dioscuri?"

"The twins Castor and Pollux together were known as Dioscuri. They were the gods of horses, and they also represent our zodiac sign —Gemini."

"What is the other one?"

"Vulcan."

"Vulcan's Greek name is Hephaestus, and he is the god of fire."

37

THE EAST COAST OF SICILY

As we went around the island it became obvious that the Greeks seemed to have preferred the east coast of Sicily as evidenced by the temples and theaters in nearly every town and city. For instance, Syracuse was hailed as a second Athens. The city was founded in 734 –733 BC by the Corinthians. And the nucleus of the ancient city was situated on the small island of Ortigia. According to Cicero, Syracuse was "the greatest Greek city and the most beautiful of them all." Syracuse is the birthplace of the great mathematician Archimedes.

"Was Archimedes the one who said, 'Give me a spot to stand on and I will move the earth?'" asked Leah.

"Yes."

He is also the one whose principle was that "a body immersed in fluid loses weight equal to the water displaced, from which one can calculate the volume of the body." He discovered this while he was having a bath. According to oral history, he forgot that he was naked and ran out into the street, exposing himself and his theory to the public. He shouted "HeuriKa'"(I have found it). One wonders what the people thought he had found!

The city was the greatest power in the Mediterranean. It exercised its supremacy all over the Magna Graecia. However, democracy did not take root on the Greek city-state of Syracuse as it did in Greece itself. Until it became part of the Roman Republic and Byzantine Empire, it had some twenty-four tyrants. Eventually, Palermo took over as the capital of the Kingdom of Sicily. Ultimately, the kingdom was united with the Kingdom of Naples to form the Two Sicilies until the Italian unification of 1860.

We must not forget, though, that Syracuse is not only famous for its pagan history, because the Christian life is also very illustrious. For instance, the people of Syracuse speak with pride that Paul of Tarsus, better known as Saint Paul, went there. On his way to Rome and coming from Malta, in Acts 28: 11–12 we read as follows:

> After three months we put out to sea in a ship that had wintered in the island—it was an Alexandrian ship with the figurehead of the twin gods Castor and Pollux. We put in at Syracuse and stayed there three days.

"So, Saint Paul traveled in a boat which had the figureheads of the pagan gods Castor and Pollux, also named Dioscuri?" asked Leah.

"It appears so. There are many myths surrounding the gods. It seems that they were also the gods of the shipwrecked."

"That's unusual," exclaimed Natalie, "that Saint Paul, who went from place to place to preach Christianity, should be traveling in a boat with a pagan figurehead of the twin gods of Castor and Pollux."

"Yes, but we must remember that Christianity was in its very early inception, and that Saint Paul was taken to Rome as a prisoner. So, he would not have had much of a choice which boat he traveled in."

"Never mind. I have made you digress, Mamma. Please continue with the Sicilians saints."

"Please, Nonna, continue.

"OK, then. Another important saint is Saint Lucy. Saint Lucy was born in Syracuse of noble family. She is not only worshipped by Catholics, but also by most Christian religions and all European countries. Saint Lucy is the patron saint of Syracuse as Saint Rosalie is of Palermo and Saint Agatha is of Catania. There are at least thirty saints in Sicily, and they are born and bred Sicilians with fascinating life stories. They are stories of amazing love and total commitment to God.

"There is a church in Syracuse, however, that it is worth mentioning. The church's architecture is considered unusual, to say the least. This is the opinion not just of the people like me but of architects from different parts of the world. The Sanctuary of Our Lady of Tears of Syracuse is called "Our Lady of Tears," because a picture of Mary in it wept for about five days consecutively for everyone to see. After all the expert analysis of the tears, it confirmed something that was already known by the faithful—that they were human tears. It was hailed a miracle. As it is well known in Italy, where there is a miracle, there has to be a church to enclose the miracle.

"And so it was! A church had to be built. It was decided to employ experts from outside Italy for the work. I don't know why this was so. Could it be that the Sicilians, at times suffer from some inferiority complex? I personally doubt it. However, whether this is possible or not, the fact remains that instead of the Sicilians doing the design for the church themselves, they called a couple of Frenchmen to do it. This will always remain a mystery to me. Anyway, the work for the creation of the church was given to Michel Arnault and Pierre Parat. Did they have the best idea? The Sicilians must have thought so."

It seems to me that the Frenchmen must have come up with the idea that the church should represent the miracle. And so, the church of Syracuse does not resemble any other church we have ever known. The church is nothing like the Norman, the medieval, the baroque, the Renaissance, and the Gothic churches, which majestically stand in their glory all over Italy, not at all. Instead, we have a church in the shape of a giant teardrop. It is as if the church had to encapsulate all the tears shed by the Madonna and the tears profusely and continuously shed by the public. In fact, one has only to enter the church to feel that one has joined the tearful assemblage.

What an amazing feeling!

38

HEPHAESTUS FURNACE

We had visited most of the towns and cities of the southeast coast of Sicily, and now we were traveling toward the north. Soon I would have to confront the past of my young life—the life of the young and yet adult Marianna. Confronting the past can be both exciting and painful. I had decided that to deal with, at times, a difficult present, it was necessary to lock my childhood away in the furthest and deepest corners of my mind.

I was Sicilian, no question about that, but when people asked me if I was proud to be a Sicilian, I did not understand why anyone should be proud of one's birthplace. How could I be proud about something I had nothing to do with? Similarly, why should I be proud of living in Australia? Yet again I had nothing to do with that. I could be proud of my achievements, but not with something about which I had no choice, and in both cases I had had no choice. These were my erratic thoughts as we were driving toward the north. Soon we would have a full view of the volcano Etna, and that would be an amazing experience for my family.

"I know we have seen Etna from a distance nearly from all over Sicily, but we should see it closer soon," stated Leah.

As we turned the corner on the road, I said, "Turn left." They all shrilled with excitement and agreed that it was much bigger than they had thought.

It was a majestic beauty, both terrifying and awesome. It looked so powerful that one felt that it dominated the whole island.

"Does it erupt often?"

"Yes, quite often. Actually, you might witness an eruption soon."

"How do you know, Nonna?" Jane sounded fearful.

"I felt the earth tremble slightly a few minutes ago."

"We didn't feel anything." They all agreed they didn't.

"You have to be in tune with the island—and then you will feel the tremor. It is as if the volcano is letting you know before it erupts.

"I suppose one has to be a Sicilian for that." Leah smiled.

"Yes, of course."

We stopped at the town of Acitrezza, and as we were walking toward a shop, Leah said, "Nonna, I felt … I felt it."

"You felt what?" asked Jane, grabbing her mother.

"I felt the tremor."

"Welcome to Sicily." For the next couple of nights, you are going to see the most spectacular fireworks you have ever seen," I said, smiling. The only other person smiling was Michael.

"Don't worry," he said, "it's not dangerous. Only once I read that the lava hit Catania. I think it was in 122 BC."

"Once it reached around here also. The hard black stone you see over there is volcanic lava. But don't worry—it doesn't happen anymore. They have actually deviated the path of lava now."

"There are a few stories about Etna also."

"Are they frightening?" asked Jane.

"No, they are not frightening."

"Tell us, Nonna. Tell us the stories.

"Have you ever heard of Typhon?"

"No, who is he?"

"Apparently, he is the hundred-head monster. He was vanquished by Zeus's thunderbolts and buried under the volcano

Etna, where the eruptions are said to be, and they are Typhon's struggles to free himself. There seems to be quite a crowd under Etna."

"Why, who else is there?" They all seemed interested in what I had to say.

"You remember Hephaestus, the god of fire? We have spoken about him. He was the son of Zeus and Hera and lived on Mount Olympus. After a quarrel with his parents, he was flung from the mount of the gods and it is said that, because of the huge fall that took days, he was hurt and became a kind of a comic figure because of his limping. I guess a limping god is not a good look.

"Anyway, it is said that he was also a blacksmith. So, he has a forge and works under Mount Etna, helped by the Cyclops. The Cyclops are giants who, according to mythology, have one eye in the middle of their foreheads. One of the Cyclops is the son of Poseidon (Neptune) and his name is Polyphemus. There are many stories told about Polyphemus. The one told by Homer in Odyssey has the giant Polyphemus hurling huge rocks after Odysseus (Ulysses), who had blinded him. The stones are the seven 'Scogli de' Ciclopi' or Faraglioni of volcanic material and are about seventy meters high, as you can see in the sea."

"Are they those over there? They are huge."

"Yes, they are."

"The other story of Polyphemus is that he fell in love with a Greek sea nymph named Galatea. Unfortunately, though, Galatea was in love with the Sicilian shepherd Aci. Polyphemus, out of jealousy, killed Aci. Galatea turned her lover's body into a freshwater river. The river flows down the slopes of Mount Etna. They say that at times you can see the water of the river turn red. No doubt that's Aci's blood. So anytime that Galatea misses Aci, she can throw herself into the river. At this stage, I don't know how one ends the story. Did they die and live happily ever after? Or is one water and the other can wash herself in him, and one is clean while the other is murky and brown and appears red and bloody? Or yet another version could be that when Galatea throws herself into the river, Aci becomes excited and flows faster down the slope. Who knows?

"You must understand that we Sicilians do not tell a story like the rest of the world. In most cases people look for evidence and then deduce what the story might have been. I guess, it is like what happens in a court case: first the evidence and then the judgment and convictions. As I said it seems that we do things the other way: first the conviction, then the judgment, and then we make up the evidence that suits the judgment and the conviction."

At this stage, the only thing I heard was, "Oh, Marianna!"

"Oh, Mamma!

"Oh, Nonna!"

The only one who wasn't laughing was Jane.

"Aci's story is such a sad story," she grumbled.

"By the way, to honor Aci, we have at least nine towns at the foot of Mount Etna that begin with the name of 'Aci', such as: Acitrezza, Acireale, Aci Castello, Aci Catena, Aci S. Filippo, Aci Platani, Aci S. Lucia, Aci Bonaccorsi and Aci Sant'Antonio. All of this never ceases to amaze me. From the Saints Filippo, Lucia, and Antonio back to Aci, the little mythological shepherd. To make a little shepherd great and immortal, the names of saints, who are great and immortal, were used to name the towns and give Aci the immortality that he might have deserved. Astuteness was obviously used here to procure the evidence to support the judgment. I rest my case."

39

THE RIVIERA OF THE CYCLOPS

Sitting in this magnificent place, an alfresco restaurant across the riviera, eating delicious food and fantasizing about distant times and the not-so-distant times, was an experience we would never forget. Looking at the Faraglioni, the huge volcanic rocks in the sea, another memory surfaced. Not of a mythological creature but of a person remembered by history. Of course, there are many famous writers in Sicily, but there is one who's my favorite. In his case the evidence speaks clearly of his greatness.

"Who's that person, Nonna?"

"That person is Giovanni Verga. He was born in Catania in 1840 into an affluent family. He is an Italian realist (verismo) writer."

"The setting of one of his books is exactly here," I said, pointing out to the coast.

"The coast that we see is called, predictably, Riviera of the Cyclops. The style of the book that Verga himself defines is to make sure that the reader 'comes face-to-face with the forthright and naked fact, without trying to find it within the lines of the book through the writer's glasses.' The book deals with a family of fishermen. The family nucleus, which appears strong at first, gradually breaks down. The strength of the family is a survival factor for Sicilians. However, in search for material well-being, the family is struck by one calamity after another. These calamities create the annihilation and the destruction of the family nucleus."

"That sculpture in the piazza is Verga. I read the dedication."

"Yes, it is. Also, the high relief on that wall is about Verga's book. Mimmo M. Lazzaro did the sculpture. It is a representation of the women waiting for their families—the fishermen who are at sea in the middle of a tempest."

"They look worried," said Jane.

"Of course, they are worried. Their families are in danger," answered Leah. Then looking at the sculpture she asked, "What does that writing at the bottom of the sculpture of the women say? What is the translation in English, Nonna?"

"'Those poor people seemed like souls of purgatory.'" I said with a sigh.

"Nonna, you like Verga very much, don't you?"

"Yes, I do. What he says in the introduction of his book applies a little to my family and to many families who went in search of other places for something better. He calls this a kind of 'restlessness for the pursuit of prosperity.' The realization that one can live better and the yearning to discover the unknown brings disruption to a family who until then had lived relatively happy."

"Your family was not poor, Nonna."

"No, you're right, Jane. However, there are other reasons why people feel restless. My father's pursuit was not prosperity, but that of trying to find peace and tranquility for himself and his family in a distant land."

"Did he find that?"

"Yes, he did."

We were eating in a leisurely way and enjoying our delicious meal when the earth trembled once more, this time a little stronger than before. Everyone felt the tremor. The girls jumped to their feet.

"We're too close to Etna, let's go away," said Jane.

"It's probably too close to the volcano anywhere on the island," replied Leah.

Leah was not that far wrong, I thought. Out loud I said, "Yes, let's leave."

"Come on girls, it is best to reach the hotel before dark," said Michael to placate the already nervous family unit.

We went north to reach our hotel. Mount Etna was already letting out smoke, but the girls didn't notice. I too wanted to go away from this place because the amazing volcano seemed to emanate a kind of threat, especially for those who observed this phenomenon for the first time.

As we were distancing ourselves from Etna and saying goodbye to the famous Riviera of the Cyclops, there was a sigh of relief. We had reached a distance where one felt almost safe. We had left Mount Etna behind. However, I was sure that soon it would reappear, and the vision of it would be unimaginable.

It was twilight, and in Sicily that lasted quite a while. With any luck, we would reach Taormina before it became dark. The road toward the town, which was on a high hill, was precarious, to say the least. The curves of the narrow road were risky during the day, not to mention at night. So, we were anxious to do our climb before darkness descended upon us. Fortunately, there were no buses at this time of the day or else it would have been quite an undertaking to try to pass them. Either the car or the bus could be pushed downhill. The thoughts and visions I was having made me quiver.

Finally, we arrived at our prebooked destination. It was getting dark, so we had to wait to see the amazing scenery tomorrow. However, that was another vista that would astound us.

As soon as Jane said, "We have lost Mount Etna," as if by magic it appeared in front of us.

"If you are in Sicily, it seems that you cannot lose Mount Etna for long," replied Leah.

I had seen Mount Etna when I was growing up in Sicily, but it had never taken my breath away as it was doing now. They do say that Sicilians hardly ever noticed the volcano. I guess one becomes accustomed to one's surroundings. One has to go away from one's environment to learn to appreciate what for a period of time was lost. Seeing Etna erupting and flames of fire, which appeared to be touching the sky, brought to mind something that Pindaro, the Greek poet, wrote in his Pitica in 470 BC: "Smoking Etna, a pillar of the sky, eternally fed by sparkling snow, whose fabric roars from the purest source of terrifying fire."

To try to describe the volcano one has to use both negative and positive words like awe-inspiring, breathtaking, splendid, fascinating, tremendous, terrifying, frightening, and so on. But even such words could never describe the underlying, inexplicable mystery that is Etna. Throughout the ages, Etna has been considered the forge of Zeus, and the realm of Hades, which, according to legend, was just below.

The fire sparkled and splattered all over the place, or so it seemed. The girls were speechless. They had realized that from here they could watch the explosive fireworks without being endangered by them. I watched Mount Etna through the eyes of my family, and it was as if I was seeing the spectacular vision for the first time. As Virgil said:

> A spreading bay is there, impregnable
> To all invading storms; and Aetna's throat
> With roar of frightful ruin thunders nigh.
> Now to the realm of light it lifts a cloud
> Of pitch-black, whirling smoke, and fiery dust,
> Shooting out globes of flame, with monster tongues
> That lick the stars; now huge crags of itself,
> Out of the bowels of the mountain torn,
> Its maw disgorges, while the molten rock
> Rolls screaming skyward; from the nether deep
> The fathomless abyss makes ebb and flow.

Whether the description of Mount Etna was made by an author of 450 BC like Pindaro or by Virgil in his Aeneid written between 29–19 BC, or perhaps, even by the onlookers of the twenty-first century, there is a similarity in the description. The language obviously differs throughout the ages, but the content appears similar like: "source of terrifying fire" or "shooting out globes of flame, with monster tongues." Or by Jane of the twenty-first century, who excitedly shouted, "Look everyone, the fire is touching the sky."

We walked and talked in amazement about what we were seeing in front of us. The street, which was facing the volcano, appeared all lit up. Eventually, we went to the hotel for the night. Tomorrow would hold other discoveries and other excitement.

The sun was shining, and it appeared that it was going to be a wonderful day.

I could hear that the girls were already up and anxious to see the town in the daylight. As we went around, there was a wonderful smell of the many pasteccerie with their diverse sweets being freshly baked. Not to mention the magnificent mouth-watering brioches. We looked at one another, and as usual Michael appeared to read our minds.

"Who's for granita and brioche?" he asked.

"We all are," we answered in unison.

We sat outside the coffee bar and were served the granita and the brioches. We dunked, as is done, the pieces of the brioches in the granita and enjoyed every delightful morsel of the summery Sicilian breakfast. The scenery was breathtaking. We could see Naxos, the most ancient of the Greek colonies. It seems that it was founded even before Syracuse, in about 735 BC. L'Isola Bella (the Beautiful Island) was also visible.

"Nonna, that island is very tiny," said Jane, pointing toward the beautiful island.

"Yes, it is. Apparently not very many people live there. I think it is privately owned."

40

DAZZLING COLORS

The brilliant colors dazzled the eyes, and the beauty of the scenery is indescribable. The green of the island, the golden sunshine glistering on the bright blue water, is a vision beyond compare. So many cultures had contributed to make this place what it is: the Greeks, the Byzantines, the Arabs, and the Normans, who reinstated the Christian religion, and the Spanish, when eventually Sicily was unified with Italy.

As we went farther up the mountain to visit the Greek theater, everything grew in magnificence, but perhaps I should let Goethe describe the amazing ancient beauty.

The proscenium was built in a diagonal at the foot of the tiered half-circle, stretching from cliff to cliff to complete a stupendous work of Art and Nature. If one sits down where the topmost spectator sat, one has to admit that no audience in any other theatre ever beheld such a view ... Straight ahead one sees the long ridge of Etna, to the left the coast line as far as Catania or even Syracuse, and the whole panorama is capped by the huge, fuming, fiery mountain ... If one turns around ... one sees two cliffs and, between them, the road winding its way to Messina.

We went around Taormina and found that every corner had something striking to offer. The ancient buildings, the beautiful baroque fountain in Piazza del Duomo, churches and the cathedral. Even though the architecture was built in different ages and by different cultures, everything came together in what appeared a harmonious work of art.

We spent a lazy day admiring the landscape, looking in the shops, and savoring the delicious food. And when the sunset came and evening was slowly becoming night and the lights were lit, the view was not any less enchanting than during the day.

No one wanted to go to bed that night. We did not want to miss anything that the place had to offer. But tomorrow we would have to start early to reach the other destination. The following morning, as we were left, we looked back with sadness.

"I will never forget this place," said Natalie.

"Nor I," replied the girls. The men nodded in agreement.

The feeling that we all liked the place was unanimous. Perhaps, another time we would come back again. Up we went to a place where I lived my childhood days.

Was I happy? I wasn't sure. Maybe I was a little anxious to see some of the people who had been kind to me. Were they still alive? I did not know. As the years went by and with the vicissitudes of life, we had lost touch with most of the people who had been an important part of my early years.

As we were traveling on the coast of the famous sea, memories kept on flooding in my mind. I could visualize the Mediterranean full of warships as they approached the shores of Sicily. History of the distant past learned at school also came to mind. Through the centuries, there would have been ships of people of different nationalities and creeds, but of the same intention—to conquer the island. And conquer they did. So many memories!

Without realizing it, we had arrived in front of the Archipelago of the Tyrrhenian Sea.

"Look girls, the Aeolian Islands," I said, pointing out toward the famous archipelago.

"Look at all the islands in the middle of the sea!" exclaimed Jane.

"That's why they are islands—they are in the middle of the sea. Sicily is an island surrounded by the sea," retorted Leah.

"I know that. Who doesn't know that?" Jane said sharply. And turning to me, she asked, "Do you know the names of the Islands, Nonna?"

"Yes, I do."

"What are they?"

"Lipari, Vulcano, Salina, Panarea, Stromboli, Alicudi, and Filicudi. A long time ago I met someone who came from Salina. Her name was Lina."

"Where did you meet her?"

"On the ship going to Australia. She was going to Australia to meet her husband, whom she had never met."

"What do you mean she had never met him?"

"She had seen him in a photograph and had married him by proxy." As soon I said that I realized that I should not have, for the questions came from left, right, and center.

"She married without the husband being there?"

"How could she do that?"

"Did she love him?"

"I asked myself the same questions. Apparently, her family was very poor, so she was forced to find a way to help herself and her family. Unfortunately, love did not even come into the equation."

I looked at Michael and felt sorry for the young girl who most probably had sacrificed her life. I hoped she had come to love the husband she had never met. I had been so fortunate to find such a selfless and mutual love. As always, Michael could read my mind. He held my hand, which had the power to change my sadness into joy.

"Have you seen that lady, Nonna?"

"She went to live somewhere in eastern Australia, so we never had the chance to see one another. To tell the truth, I had forgotten about her until now. When life guides people toward different directions, regrettably it is easy to forget someone you had met for a brief moment in time."

41

A Clear Day

As we were driving along the coast, it seemed as if the Aeolian Archipelago was moving with us. We had such a clear vision of the islands that their distance seemed closer to the coast of Sicily since the last time I had seen them.

However, that was a very long time ago, and as a young girl I did not have the fascination or the appreciation for the scenery as I had now as an adult. When I was young, I tried to imagine what was beyond the horizon, and my gaze must have ignored what was close to me. Now I knew what was on the other side of the world, so I could look closely and see, to a certain extent, what I had missed before. As I was getting closer to the place where I had lived, memories kept on flooding my mind.

As I was admiring the islands, I remembered Carmela. Carmela was the "servant," or so my family called her. I, on the other hand, loved her as a member of my family, which did not please my family very much, but I did not take much notice of that. I did not like pompous people very much, even if those people were members of my family. I had learned so much from Carmela; she had an amazing knowledge that was passed on orally through the ages. As far as I knew, she had never learned to read or write, but she could recite poems, recount mythology, relate history, quote the greats like Dante, and narrate stories from bestselling authors, not to mention her knowledge of current affairs. How did she do it? She listened— she was able to hear and comprehend behind closed doors.

Actually, most of the Sicilian people were great storytellers, especially the women—the elderly grandmothers who told us enchanting mythological stories that eventually found their way into books. Prehistorical tales were something to look forward to on a cold winter's night; the land covered with snow created an atmosphere for nymphs, witches and fairies. Gathered around the fire, eating chestnuts, and listening to the captivating fairy tales was the ultimate joyful pastime. I remember being transported into another realm of supernatural and magical creatures that came together with celestial and angelic beings. Looking back into our childhood one can see that with a youthful imagination anything becomes possible.

When I was a child, I loved to hear the people reciting and singing stories to either vituperate some family who had committed something scandalous or praise some other who had done something well. Needless to say, the people who had done something immoral or shameful attracted a larger audience. The Greeks, no doubt, had bequeathed this practice to Sicily, since Homer the great author of Iliad, was thought to be a bard.

I was so immersed in my childhood memories that I had not heard the family addressing me until Michael asked:

"Are you OK, Marianna? You seemed deep in thought."

"Yes, I am fine. I was remembering things of long ago, things that I had thought forgotten have surfaced in my memory as if it were yesterday."

"Nonna, the Aeolian Islands look so beautiful. They are so clear against the blue sky," said Leah.

"There is a story about that."

"There's a story about everything in Sicily. But I like a good story," said Jane.

"We all know that," replied Leah.

"What's the story?"

"It's nothing much. It's something that Carmela used to say about the Aeolian Islands when I was a child."

"What did she say?"

"She said that when you could see the Aeolian so clearly against the sky like they are today, it would soon rain."

"Everything in Sicily is the opposite of the rest of the world," said Natalie, laughing.

"Was it true? Did it rain?"

"Yes, it always did. And you are right, Natalie, many Sicilian beliefs appear to be different. For instance, the number thirteen, which is thought by many cultures to be bad luck, is believed to be good luck in Sicily."

As usual the magnificent scenery left us almost speechless, but not for long.

"Girls, look at the island closer to Sicily," I said, pointing to Vulcano. There are the fumaroles where one can bathe in warm water. There are also sulfur vapors that people use as inhalation therapy."

"Is this where Venus was supposed to have emerged from the sea?" asked Michael.

"As you know, according to the Botticelli depiction, Venus's birth was of an adult naked woman emerging from the frothy waters on a seashell, but even though the Sicilians claim many things about Venus, I have not heard that this was necessarily the sea she emerged from. There is, however, something that they say about Venus in the sea near Vulcano."

"What is that?" asked Michael.

"You know that the goddess Venus represented beauty, love, enticement, seduction, and sex. Legend has that she had children both with gods and mortals, about twenty-five offspring, I was told by the know-it-all Carmela, the family housekeeper. While Carmela discussed most things with me, she did not want me to know the other part of the conversation about Venus. According to Carmela, young people should not hear certain things. However, because the Sicilian in me made me curious, I too was learning to see the signs and hear the whispers. Anyway, I heard Carmela talking to her friend that she usually gossiped with; she said that after she had a child, Venus had to become a virgin again before she could have sex in order to have the next child."

"How did she do that?" said Michael, trying desperately not to laugh.

"Easy! She used to immerse herself in the seawater."

"And that did it?"

"Of course, why wouldn't it?"

"Was it the warm water or the emissions of sulfur that did it?"

"That I don't know. This story was passed on mouth to mouth and I don't think it has even reached the books like the other mythological tales."

"I wonder why!" said Michael. We both laughed.

"Are you going to tell this story to the girls?" he whispered.

"No, like Carmela, I think we should wait for a few years to share this astonishing Sicilian anecdote."

As we traveled along the coast, the Aeolian Archipelago seemed to travel with us.

"Have we long to go, Nonna?"

"No, a few more curves and then we should turn and follow the road to go up the mountain, I think."

"Don't you remember?"

"Yes, I remember. But don't forget, it is still a distant memory —almost the memory of another life."

42

THE RETURN

The curve where we had to turn left was in sight. Soon we would leave the coast behind to climb toward the town where I had spent part of my early youth.

"Another mountain to climb," said Raymond, who was driving.

"Actually, by Sicilian standards, this is not a mountain but a hill; a high hill, but a hill nevertheless."

"Did you travel up and down this hill when you lived in Sicily, Nonna?"

"Yes, many times. We used to take the bus any time that we had to catch the train."

"Does a bus fit around these curves on the road?"

"Yes, Jane, but it becomes difficult when a bus meets another bus or another car, for that matter."

As soon as I said that I regretted it, because we could see a car coming around the corner. I think everyone held their breath, me included. It was a long time since I had traveled this road, and when the car went past ours, to my relief and, no doubt, Raymond's, the passed without hitting or scraping one another. The alternative would be a titanic spiraling down into the ravine. I looked at my family and trembled with fear. As always, Michael appeared to know my thoughts, for he put his arm around me. As usual, my imagination was getting the better of me. I should not allow such ideas to clutter my mind, because deep down I knew that thoughts could be erratic and unreliable and therefore unpredictable. "Do not believe all that you think." I heard that said many times.

I relaxed a little and tried to enjoy the wonderful view. I tried to remember the places as we went toward the town where I spent my school days, some distance away from where the Del Feo family lived. I looked at the humongous trees on the side of the road, but I did not recognize the landscape. Perhaps, the trees had grown as I had and had become unrecognizable, as I would be to the people I used to know.

The people I used to know? Who was gone? I had left this place a lifetime ago, and the people who were elderly had surely passed on to the next life. Suddenly I realized that my return would not be a joyous occurrence but a very painful one. Distant memories kept on flooding my mind. I thought of Sara and Peppe, the settlers who looked after our land and who had been my mentors. Carmela, who was uneducated and yet had an innate knowledge of everything. She was thought by everyone to be an ignorant and good-for-nothing servant. How wrong everyone was, my family included, for judging her in such a negative way.

It was so sad to see that people acted in the way they were judged. The realization that with our judgment we had the power to make some people act with intelligence or stupidity saddened me. As a young girl, I also had used language to belittle Carmela. Fortunately, she loved me, regardless.

Suddenly, as we went around the corner, I recognized the place around us. So many times, I was told to do the sign of the cross in front of the cemetery. Automatically, without realizing, I made the sign of the cross.

Michael, looking at me, asked, "Do you remember this place?"

"Yes," I replied, "behind those trees there is a cemetery." I had tears in my eyes. "Around the other curve, we will see the town."

"Are you looking forward to seeing the people you know?"

"Yes and no, because while I can see the place that I knew so well, I do not think that I will see many people I knew and loved."

Suddenly, the sun was shining, taking away the darkness caused by the shadow of the huge trees.

"There it is, girls, the town where I went to school. Very soon we will be in the piazza where young people spent time together."

"Look, Nonna! We can see Etna again," said Leah. Seeing Etna made the girls excited. The piazza was the same as I remembered except that it was almost empty. The young people who came together to get away from the family were nowhere to be seen. The few people that we did see were strangers to me. There was one person, however, who kept on waving to us, and most especially to me.

"He is waving at you. Go and meet him." Michael was smiling.

Suddenly, as I realized who the person was, my heart started to pound. We ran toward one another and embraced. Years of distance were obliterated. We were children once again.

43

A Blast from the Past

"You are the only friend I ever had here in Sicily, Mariana."

"We are more than friends; we are cousins."

"That's what I mean. You were the only person who accepted me as your cousin."

"That's Sicily for you. A beautiful place and most of the time a generous people, but things are remembered for generations."

"You did not think that. You always treated me as your cousin and not as your 'bastard cousin' like everyone else."

"I would never think that of you. You were, after all, my grandfather's grandson. According to the law, you are my half-cousin and not my bastard cousin."

"But let's forget this nonsense. Tell me what you have done with your life. I know that you are married with two beautiful children, but I don't know much else. Is your wife Sicilian?

"No, my wife is not Sicilian. I met her in Switzerland."

"You have been working in Switzerland"?

"Yes, thanks to you."

"What do you mean thanks to me? I haven't done anything. I live on the other side of the world."

"I do not mean now, but when we were young children. Remember when you said that it was important for me to go to school, and I told you that even at a young age, I had to work because my family was very poor. You told me that you knew that there was a night school. The government had recently made a night school possible for the children who were unable to go during the day. And so, I went to the night school and learned to read and write. As a result, I was able to get a decent job."

"Are you in Sicily on holiday or to visit someone?"

As my family was coming toward us, he replied, "Yes, I am here to visit someone. You and your family."

"How did you know that we were here?" He looked at my husband and smiled. I realized that Michael had let Basilio know that we were coming to Sicily. My husband never ceased to amaze me. I smiled and said, "You have a chance to meet my family, Basilio."

"Is every member of your family here?"

"No, my younger daughter is back in Australia."

"Everyone, meet our cousin Basilio."

They all hugged and kissed and asked questions. In particular, they wanted to know when he was going back to Switzerland.

"Tomorrow," he replied.

I was astounded. "I thought we could have a few days together."

"I wish I could stay longer, but I can't. Work awaits me."

We spent a wonderful day together. We reminisced on time gone by. We walked around the piazza, and we admired the wonderful panorama. I remembered that this town was surrounded by twenty-five towns, all situated on hills and mountains with magnificent green valleys and a river running through.

"What a magnificent vista. We have never seen anything more spectacular." The family agreed. "Who would not want to live here?" They all looked at me.

The day was filled with joy. We drank excellent coffee and ate wonderful sweets that Sicily is famous for. Not to mention the scrumptious meals we ate. As darkness descended upon us and the lights went on, we could see clearly the towns that surrounded us. The beauty was indescribable. Michael was looking at me; he could sense the emotion I felt. He probably wondered if the choice that he had left to me to make was already made. The choice was in the making but, perhaps, it was not what he thought I would be making.

The following morning, we said goodbye to Basilio. He promised that he and his family would come and visit us. Basilio had been like a brother to me, especially because there wasn't any other member of the family that accepted him. I felt immense compassion for him. I was happy, though, that he had a family that loved him. Hearing how much he adored and was adored by his wife and children made me happy. He deserved to be loved and to receive respect, because he, most definitely, did not deserve anything else.

Basilio was the only person I had met and knew. Thus far, I did not know anyone else I had seen in the piazza. Everyone I saw was a total stranger to me. Perhaps, when we went to see the property that we had, I would see someone I used know. I already felt a stranger in a place where I had been loved and respected.

Off we went to where the Del Feo family used to live. As we approached the place, I saw that the road had been made larger and where I used to ride my horse, young people now drove their cars. When we reached the huge house where we lived, the girls were amazed at the size of the mansion.

"You and your family lived here, Nonna?"

"Yes," I replied, with sadness in my voice.

"Are you crying, Nonna?"

"No, not really."

I was, in fact, trying to hold back my sadness. Things were so different when I lived here. I wondered who had bought the house. A voice told me that soon I would find out.

"I know you. You are Baronessa Del Feo." I smiled; it had been years since I had been called that.

"Call me Marianna," I replied. "I think I remember you too." I knew, however, that she would never have called me by my first name. Sicily and the Sicilians had not changed that much.

"Yes, my father was one of your colono. He spoke so well of you. He used to say that you treated your workers with respect and in return everyone esteemed you."

"I learned so much from them. Your father taught me how to plant vegetables, and I have planted them in Australia. Every time I did that, I remembered him with deep affection."

"How wonderful! My father would have loved to hear that. But unfortunately, he is not with us any longer." And then changing the subject, which I could see was still hurting her, she said, "Could we have the honor of you and your beautiful family to have coffee with my family?" She was gazing at and studying each member of my family.

I introduced them and replied, "The honor will be all ours." I looked at my family to make sure that everyone was happy to accept the invitation. They all nodded.

"We are happy to have coffee with you and your family," I replied.

As we went into the house, memories of a childhood, came to mind. We met Annetta's family and the young girls who were on holiday from the University of Palermo. Things were definitely changing in Sicily. They were doing what I would have done had I stayed in Sicily. I was happy for them because they could make their dreams come true.

With their graduation they would able to change their family's status. Status was something important to my family, but most definitely not to me. My university years were important to me for learning and not to be thought greater than anyone else. The young people told us what they wanted to achieve with their degrees and soon there would be lawyers and doctors in the family. I could see how proud their mother was, and that made me happy for her and all of them.

The house was the same as we had left it. Annetta told us that they had bought only a small section of it. The enormous house was divided into apartments.

"Otherwise, people could not afford to buy the whole mansion," she said.

We complimented her on the wonderful sweets she served with the coffee. I said that I remembered that the members of her family were great cooks, and that I had tasted the beautiful biscotti they used to make.

After a very pleasant afternoon, we said our goodbyes. She made us promise that we would come back to visit her and her family once again.

"You can come and see us when you visit your aunt. I know that she went out this morning, and she would not be home just yet."

"So, I have just one aunt left?" I never thought I would visit any of them because my memory of what they had done to my mother and me, even after so many years, was still vivid in my mind. There was no doubt though; I would have to see her when I went to see the other people.

We went back to the hotel where we were staying, with the intention of coming back the next day. Natalie did not know the sordid story that, as a child, I had witnessed what my father's sisters had done to my mother, but she guessed by my demeanor that I did not particularly like my auntie and that there had been a good reason for that. But I could not explain that my three aunties, plus a friend of theirs, had very nearly killed my mother, and that my mother had felt dishonored and sick, physically and mentally, for the rest of her life.

44

Past Sadness

Past sadness was still hurting in the present. My aunt ran to me
and hugged me. I cringed and quivered. The past was now present.
It had brought with it the childhood sorrow. For a moment I had
become the seven-year-old girl who had lost her childhood and had
become an adult who was always afraid of being hurt. But then I
looked around and saw my family, and especially my wonderful
loving and adoring husband who would do anything for me and vice
versa—and was reassured.

I was a different person now. I had become a courageous person,
a resolute person that one becomes when she or he has to adopt a
different way of life in a different country. To survive this encounter
with this person I had to distance myself from her. My auntie was
hugging and kissing me; she was telling everyone how much she
loved me and that I was her favorite niece. What a lot of balderdash!
I thought.

I wanted to escape the embrace, and in order to do so, I looked at the crowd around us to see whether I could recognize some person—any person—who would tear me away from the grip that I was locked in. However, there was no one in sight that I recognized. No doubt, everyone knew who I was, but I had no idea who all those people were. Most probably I would find out later, when I was released from the clutch that was restraining me.

As usual, Natalie was able to perceive my discomfort and whispered, "She wants to be forgiven, Mamma."

Whether this was true or not, it did not matter; I had to be the person to try to leave the past where it belonged—in the past. She invited us to go to dinner at her place and I politely replied that our time was limited, and we could not go. "Perhaps another time." She seemed pleased with my reply.

Suddenly I saw someone I recognized. I ran to her, and we embraced. We had gone to school together. "Is that you, Marianna?"

"Yes, it's me."

She asked me if I had come back to Sicily to stay. But before I could reply, a group of her friends pulled her away. I realized that my spot with my friends had been filled. Did that upset me? Not really! Life had taken everyone away in different directions. I also had made friends on the other side of the world. I was hoping that the following day, I would meet friends of mine. Perhaps, since the next day we are going to see some of the land that we owned, it will be like old times, I will see people I knew, I thought. The people who had bought the land had said that if we came back, we could visit the property and buy it back if we wanted to.

We went back to the piazza in the town where we were staying and found out that a family that apparently was related to the Del Feo family had been looking for us. They had heard that we were in town and wanted to meet us. I was happy that finally I could meet relatives of mine. And there they were, running toward us. They took us for coffee, and as we talked, we realized that we were distant cousins, but cousins, nevertheless. In Sicily one could be seven times removed, but you were still cousins!

"The people in the whole of Sicily are cousins, then," said Jane.

"Perhaps," I replied. We all laughed. After our relatives left us, we went for a walk. It was a beautiful evening.

Suddenly, Leah said, "I feel the ground moving under my feet." I had felt it also, but I wasn't going to say anything. I did not want to worry anyone.

As a girl, I had felt these earth tremors many times, and I was almost used to them. We had felt some tremors already, but this was slightly stronger. Since I never felt earthquakes in Australia, it was different now; suddenly I felt quite nervous. Of course, I had to say something to reassure the girls that tremors like the one that they could feel happened many times in Sicily.

"Look over there," I said, pointing out toward Etna. "The volcano is erupting again, and as it throws the lava out, the earth trembles. Remember what I said to you? Hephaestus must be angry and has lit a huge fire and made the ground shake." They all laughed. What I had intended to happen, did. We all looked at the volcano and saw the smoke coming out of it.

The movement of the ground stopped, and Jane said: "Hephaestus is not so angry anymore and, perhaps he has gone to sleep." We all laughed and very soon the incident was almost forgotten. We kept on walking, looking at the magnificent and wonderful panorama.

The following day, I woke up feeling a little apprehensive. "Would I see people I knew, and would they remember me?" In a place where I had been loved and nurtured by wonderful people, I was gradually feeling that having gone in different directions, we had lost one another.

Actually, it was worse than that. In the morning, we started early to visit the different properties in different places. The first one had a river of freshwater emerging from the mountainside, which was directed through our property to water the different vegetables. To do that, the workers took their shoes off and worked barefoot. I did the same thing, which shocked the workers because my aristocratic family would never approve of my problematic behavior. Did I care?

I used to call this property the Garden of Eden. It had every vegetable and every fruit one could possibly think of. On our arrival at the property, I was anxious to see if there was someone, anyone, of the people I used to know. As we went through the place, I realized that the Garden of Eden had been defaced, and the house where my dear friends, Sara and Peppe had lived was dilapidated. No one could possibly live in it. The devastation I was seeing I also felt within me.

My Garden of Eden had become the gehenna. Michael realized that my desolation was intense. Without saying anything, he put his arms around me, and without shame, I sobbed. My family realized that my beautiful property was now a horrid mess, a place where everyone threw their waste. Not a human being was in sight. All the other properties were no different. "Let's go home," I whispered.

"Has Nonna made her choice?" Jane asked her mother.

"Perhaps she has," replied her mother.

45

ANOTHER PLACE, ANOTHER TIME

When we left our beautiful island with its wonderful people, I had been devastated. I thought that my father did not consider us, his children. We had a right to make a choice about our lives. It was OK for parents to instruct and teach their children about manners and decency, but it was not all right to upend their lives, I had often thought.

After the war there was much poverty in Sicily, and people were migrating to different parts of the world. However, our family was not poor and could live without concerns. My father had chosen Australia because it was the furthest continent from Europe and it would not be touched by war. Was it the real reason? Or, perhaps, he wanted to get away from his family, in particular his wayward sisters who had almost destroyed his wife's life.

My father's side of the family was not as noble as my mother's side. Of course, I would never know the true reason why we moved everything that we had and everything that we were, to live in a country that we knew little, if anything, about. Similarly, Australia knew very little about us, and the little that it knew was very negative. The inability of the Italians to speak English was considered total ignorance.

As time went by, however, I became used to the new country, especially since I had learned English and was able to converse. There was no reason why I should be ridiculed anymore, I thought. The choice that my husband wanted me to make was the one that I could not make when I had come to Australia: Did I want to continue to live in Australia or did we want to return to Sicily?.

No doubt, Sicily was a beautiful place to visit, but did I want to come and live here?

Young Jane had reminded me that, going to Australia, I had thought that I had gone past a point of no return.

"That could still be true," I had replied.

"What do you mean, Nonna? Didn't you quote Dante when he said that travelers should not go over their limits?"

"Yes, he was talking about Ulysses going over boundaries, but he continued to say this:"

> Think of your breed; for brutish ignorance
> Your mettle was not made; you were made men,
> To follow after knowledge and excellence. (Dante,
> Canto XXVI)

"Does it mean that people should travel, Nonna?"

"Yes, it does. Since there is learning in traveling, people should seek 'knowledge and excellence' through traveling, among other things."

"So, you didn't reach a point of no return."

"I think I have."

"What do you mean, Nonna?"

"We will talk about this tomorrow."

The following morning Michael told me that he had to go out for a while. "I won't be long," he said. "I need some information before we have our important discussion." On his return, we went to the park to be free to have our talk. I was to tell my family my decision as to where I chose to live—Australia or Sicily. My choice had already been made. Actually, to be precise, life itself had made it for me. My family was anxious to find out what my decision would be.

"Before I tell you my decision of where I would love to live for the rest of my life, I will have to tell you something which I was too embarrassed to tell you before. So, all my life I have kept a secret from you, and for this I apologize profusely. I realized that you, my dearest family, had a right to know."

"What is it, Mamma? What's so important that you had to keep it a secret?" Natalie's voice sounded agitated.

"Please don't worry! It should not be that important, after all, but it has affected the decisions that I had to make in my life. Of course, I realize that being embarrassed is no excuse to keep secrets from the people you love. The reason why I cannot come back to live in Sicily is that I'm not an Italian citizen anymore. When I became an Australian citizen, I was forced to renounce my Italian citizenship."

"What do you mean, you were forced?"

"First of all, I did not apply to become an Australian citizen because, at the time, I hoped that we would come back home.

"However, one day a government representative called me, and I was told that I must become an Australian citizen. So, I had to decide whether I wanted to or not. But the worst part was yet to come. One night, the people who had applied to obtain their citizenship and I were gathered at the town hall. When I was asked to repeat the words after the gentleman by placing my hand on the Bible, I nearly fainted. I could not renounce my country because I would be renouncing who I was. They were taking away not only my being Italian but also who I truly was. I was devastated, to say the least; but I had my hand on the Bible, and the man kept on urging me to repeat after him. He must have been pleased with my mumbling because I went through as an Australian citizen!

"Couldn't you obtain a dual citizenship?"

"No, according to the Australian government, because I had accepted to give up my own country, and, as a result I was not considered Italian. I could not reclaim an Italian citizenship."

"This is unbelievable," said everyone in unison. "There is nothing you can do?"

"Yes, there is," replied Michael.

"There is?" I asked.

"This morning I went to the immigration office to inquire about the situation, and I was told that if you live here for three months, you will regain the Italian citizenship." Michael looked at me, and shaking his head, said, "You don't like the idea, do you?"

"It seems absurd that both countries decided that I am not who I truly am. I would have thought that from the moment I walked in the country where I was born, and they knew who my ancestors were, I would be accepted as being Italian, once again. They cannot hold against me the fact that I was literally forced to repeat words that had no meaning for me."

"The fact that you were underage when you became an Australian citizen should also be considered," said Michael.

"Please, everyone, do not think that I do not respect my Australian passport, because I do; it is the way it was obtained that I resent."

46

REPLANTED

The frail sapling was uprooted from where it had been planted, and most probably would not survive. Or so I thought, comparing myself to a fragile little plant. At first, it may have been difficult for the little plant to survive on a different soil of a different land, but it gradually stared to grow. At first it looked scrawny, but soon the sapling formed new roots and healthy branches. Gradually, it had grown into a tall and strong tree and was bearing fruit.

As a child in Sicily, I had felt one with my special tree. I would climb my favorite tall tree and look at the never-ending horizon and wonder what it was like on the other side. Looking from the tallest tree, I felt that I could overcome and conquer every obstacle.

However, my tree had been cut and did not exist anymore. Even though I felt a little sad at first, I realized that over the years, it was inevitable that changes occurred both in places and in people. I realized that I did not need the tree to wonder what was beyond the horizon anymore, because I lived there. Beyond the horizon, in the distant land of Australia, I was able to do anything I set my mind to do, and I had done just that: I had conquered many obstacles and I had achieved most of my dreams.

Here in Sicily, most of the people I knew did not exist anymore, and the ones that did had taken other directions, like I had. Finally, I realized that I could not go back to who I was and leave behind who I had become. As years went by, it was inevitable that changes had occurred. Suddenly, my decision, which had been uncertain, became obvious. The point of no return had been reached! Suddenly, Carmela's words, "people who go to Australia never come back," made sense.

"Nonna, are you OK? You look pensive," asked Leah. "Are you still worried about the decision you have to make as to where you are going to live?"

"My decision has never been problematic. Nonno wanted me to make a choice, a choice that would make me happy for the rest of my life. And since we were coming to Sicily anyway, it was a good time to see whether where I was born was the place to live. Of course, I gave much thought to the idea."

"Nonna, please tell us where you going to live." Jane sounded anxious.

"Before I tell you that, I will have to explain something. There are a few things I can do, all of which seem inappropriate."

47

CLICHÉ?

"Girls, in order to explain my feelings, I will use a phrase that may seem to be a cliché."

"I know what that is", said Jane.

"What is it, then?" asked Leah, who appeared certain that her young sister could not possibly know the meaning of the word.

To our surprise, Jane said, "A cliché is a phrase that is not original."

"A phrase or an opinion that, over the years, has been overused," continued Leah.

"This phrase, most definitely, has been overused, and probably even abused. I'm certain it has been translated into most languages. It has been around the world for over two thousand years.

It was written in AD 23 by a Roman philosopher, Gaius Plinius Secundus, better known as Pliny the Elder, who said: 'Home is where the heart is.'"

"Where is your heart, Nonna?"

"My heart is where you are, Jane, and of course, where the rest of my family is. Not forgetting my other beautiful daughter back in

Australia. The point of no return was when I had my daughters and later my granddaughters, not forgetting my wonderful son-in-law. I could not live without you, and I could not ask you to come and live with me in Italy and tear you away from the place where you were born and have become appreciated and respected. Also, I must admit that there is no place for me in Sicily. After so many years of absence from the place, I do not recognize many people, and they do not remember me. Everything that I knew belongs to another era and almost to another person."

I looked at my darling husband, and he appeared emotional. I hugged him and said: "Let's go home!" Everyone encircled us with a hug of pure joy.

Printed in the United States
by Baker & Taylor Publisher Services